John Buyers is a commercial solicitor and partner at Osborne Clarke LLP, an international law firm which specialises in advising high technology clients, or businesses that are transitioning through a process of digitalisation. John manages the UK Commercial team and leads Osborne Clarke's international Artificial Intelligence and Machine Learning group. He is a frequent commentator on the topic of Artificial Intelligence and the law and speaks regularly both in the UK and internationally on the subject.

John's practice is largely based on transactional IT and outsourcing in the Financial Services and regulated Professional Services sectors. He regularly advises users and suppliers of Artificial Intelligence based systems. Recent work has included advising a global technology business on the legal implications of automated facial recognition in Europe and providing guidance to a major social media network on the discriminatory effects of automated content takedown.

Artificial Intelligence
The Practical Legal Issues
2nd Edition

Artificial Intelligence
The Practical Legal Issues
2nd Edition

John C. Buyers, LLB Hons, MA
Solicitor England & Wales
and Republic of Ireland
Partner, Head of Commercial,
Osborne Clarke LLP

Law Brief Publishing

Published 2021 by Law Brief Publishing, an imprint of Law Brief Publishing Ltd
30 The Parks
Minehead
Somerset
TA24 8BT

www.lawbriefpublishing.com

Paperback: 978-1-912687-78-7

To Tom.

ACKNOWLEDGEMENTS

My grateful thanks go to the following people whose helpful thoughts and commentaries proved invaluable in the preparation of this work:

Dr Sanjeev B. Ahuja

Catherine Hammon

PREFACE

When I started the first edition of my book back at the end of 2017, I knew that the artificial intelligence and machine learning space would be fast moving. Little did I realise the ferocity of that pace. Since the first edition was published in the Spring of 2018 we have seen dramatic developments in pretty much all of the areas that I wrote about at that time.

Automated Facial Recognition has reached high levels of public consciousness and concern, spawned the world's first legal cases and has necessitated a completely new chapter in this second edition.

The EU seems to have dispensed with the view that legal personality for robots is a good idea. EU Commission president Ursula Von Der Leyen made AI regulation an overriding priority, but then found her grand vision stalled due to concerns from some EU member states. Whether that grand vision proceeds remains to be seen.

The increasing technological sophistication of DeepFakes (including audio DeepFakes) has turned what was at the time a technology with a relatively trivial use into a fully blown cyber security threat and in a much wider sense has stress tested our already weakened relationship with the truth.

Finally of course, the onset of the COVID-19 pandemic has changed global society and brought to the fore the impact of track and trace apps and other pandemic management technologies, many of which are powered by machine learning.

As is perhaps more than indicated in the book's title, pragmatism and utility for practitioners working in this space has always been my driving philosophy, and I am grateful for the words of praise and encouragement that the first edition received. I intend to stick to this mantra.

This book has opened doors which have in turn strengthened my network and links into the wider AI and machine learning community which have been incredibly useful in gaining insights into how practically machine learning technologies are being used and deployed.

As I mentioned in the first edition, there will always be books which will delve into these topics in more detail. Mine is intended to be the initial guide into the foothills!

The law in this edition is as stated as at 31st January 2021. As I have previously indicated, this is a new and emerging field, and there are a number of policy and legislative initiatives which could materially change the analysis in this book. It is not intended as a substitute for proper and directed legal advice. In cases of specific query, please consult with your friendly expert lawyer.

John C. Buyers
February 2021

CONTENTS

CHAPTER ONE
AN INTRODUCTION TO ARTIFICIALLY INTELLIGENT SYSTEMS

This is a book about technology and artificial intelligence – more specifically one that is designed to assist the non-scientifically minded legal practitioner to understand the implications of this new and exciting technology: to demystify, and hopefully provide clarity around the issues and implications that we as legal practitioners will need to take into account when navigating our disparate legal disciplines. It does not purport to be definitive – the technology is far too new for this and is in a state of constant evolution. What it strives to do is to provide a grounding relative to the current "state of the art" as it applies today, and separate fact from fiction.

We are currently experiencing a golden age or renaissance period for machine learning and wider artificial intelligence-based systems. This book is predominantly focussed on the innovations provided by *machine learning* – that is to say technology which, through exponential growth and scale in computing power, has enabled effective use of neural networks to enable machines to adapt and learn *without explicit programming*. It is important however not to ignore associated technologies that complement and enhance machine learning systems, and it is this wider ensemble of techniques (including machine learning itself) which I refer to as *artificial intelligence or AI*.

To the casual observer, it seems that the technology is advancing on a daily or even hourly basis. You can now talk to Alexa, Siri or Cortana using the ordinary spoken word (in whatever language is your norm) and through the miracle of natural language processing get a cogent answer, or instruct Google to run context based searches on characteristics gleaned from your photo collection. Facebook will now identify your friends and family for you and Spotify will try to define your musical tastes by selecting music tracks based on your listening history.

We're at the stage now where you can also get into your Tesla vehicle and it will drive you to your destination (albeit with your hands on the wheel). Motoring is an apt analogy, as we accelerate off into a brave new world, cosseted and nannied by ever complex varieties of AI powered gadgets. It's not all about consumer experience though. Financial markets have long been driven by a variety of robo-trading tools and many "state of the art" cyber protection systems use artificial intelligence to protect against an ever-complex world of malware.

What makes these systems different from traditional computer systems and why should we be worried? Sometimes it can be difficult to differentiate fact from fiction – particularly in an environment which is driven by marketing hype and plain old misinformation – especially so given that the idea of the intelligent machine, fuelled by Hollywood, plays heavily on our collective psyche. Is for example artificial intelligence the end of the world as we know it and are we about to be suborned to a new species of supercomputer, or is it the key to a prosperous new future and a golden age of human endeavour? This book will at least give you an oversight of the issues involved from a legal perspective, and I suspect an appreciation that the reality is somewhat more prosaic than either the pessimists or optimists would have us believe.

In order to understand the practical implications of the technology, it is worth understanding how traditional computer systems work, and analogise this against how neuroscience currently thinks that neurons in the human brain function.

Computers in the traditional sense need prescriptive and directive sets of instructions to execute complex tasks – in essence, their programming. A traditional computer is unable to handle complex tasks effectively unless every eventuality is programmed into its code. As we all know, this makes these machines highly effective at larger repetitive or data intensive tasks, with a defined set of pre-programmed variables. What such machines cannot do well is adapt, learn, evolve or extrapolate their decisions to new and unforeseen situations. In contrast, the human brain although rather less good at repetitive tasks, is a marvel of flexibility and of navigating through a chaotic world. It does this through a process of *conceptualisation*.

The simple act of recognising a human face (or indeed any image) provides a real-life example. You learn from an early age as a human being to recognise a face from any angle or orientation, full on or profile. You can identify someone in low light and you don't need an image of a face to be in colour or even in three dimensions for you to recognise it. Your brain can extrapolate a face from incomplete or partial data – indeed it is unbelievably good at "joining the dots" (so much so that we are often caught out by recognising anthropomorphic features in inanimate objects). A traditionally programmed computer finds this task almost insurmountably complex and difficult to achieve[1]. You need to ensure that the face you want the machine to recognise is oriented in precisely the right way and under precisely the right lighting conditions – as otherwise it may not even identify it as a face. In this context, what the human neocortex achieves (and what current AI technologists are trying to replicate) is the holy grail of the *"invariant representation"*. This is the ability to learn what a "face" is as a *concept* (or indeed a cube, car, tree or any other animate or inanimate thing) and apply this to real world data. The notion of a concept introduces an entirely new dimension – a level of data abstraction, classification, recognition and labelling which enables semantic representation in areas such as pattern recognition and linguistics, in short, bringing order from chaos.

Put grandly, artificially intelligent systems aspire through their structures (to a greater or lesser degree) to have the ability to process unstructured data, to extrapolate it, and to adapt and evolve in ways which are comparable to human beings.

Robotics, Perception and Artificial Intelligence

So what makes robots different from machine learning systems? It is worth briefly covering the difference as to the uninitiated, this can be a somewhat confusing question – particularly when the terms are used fast,

---

[1] This is difficulty is often referred to as Moravec's Paradox, articulated by Hans Moravec and others in 1988. He postulated that whilst it was comparatively easy to get computers to exhibit "adult" level skills, such as playing chess or checkers (draughts), it was difficult or impossible to give them the skills of a one year old in terms of perception and mobility.

loose and interchangeably in most commercial, non-technical literature.

Obviously, at its most simplistic level, a robot is a mechanism that is designed to replicate the actions and behaviours of living creatures. It is a manufactured autonomous agent in the real world which is capable of autonomous action to a defined degree. Robots in some form or another have been in existence for over 200 years[2].

As AI systems have become more sophisticated and able, robotic research has likewise developed more capable robotic machines and scientists in the field of robotics have become more pre-occupied with replicating animal characteristics of proprioception –the unconscious ability in living creatures of knowing at all times the boundaries and extent of their physical body and that when a limb is extended in front of it, it is part of its own body and has a sense of movement. Knowing also that the limb is sensing hot or cold or touching another object, and whether it is constrained or injured are an integral part of this ability in living creatures. It is this need to physically interact with the real world on an effective basis which has been described by some commentators as one of the primary catalysts of animal and human intelligence and which is the driving emphasis for AI research in the field of robotics.

A brief history of AI

Before we get into how current "state of the art" artificially intelligent systems are structured, it is worth (briefly) looking at the historical evolution of machine learning. It was Alan Turing who first coined the term "artificial intelligence", and who through his brilliant efforts in the second world war, managed to decode Nazi Germany ciphers produced on the Enigma machine. Alan Turing wrote on the concept of machine intelligence in a seminal 1950 paper[3]. His analysis centred on human intelligence as a benchmark for artificial intelligence (more on this later). He postulated that if you could hold a test where a human conversed with a computer and that human could be fooled by a clever computer

---

[2] The term robot derives from the Czech word *robota*, which means forced labour or slavery.

[3] Computing Machinery and Intelligence (1950) by A.M. Turing

program into thinking that the machine they were talking to was in fact human, then the machine would have passed a benchmark for intelligence. This of course evolved into the famous "*Turing test*".

The Turing test led to a surge in the mid 20th century in traditional programming techniques being used to emulate intelligence – however developers very soon realised the limitations of this approach. Programs such as Eliza, one of the very first early winners of a Turing test, fooled reviewers by adopting clever, but simple linguistic tricks (e.g. through the repetition of questions) which gave a superficial semblance of self-awareness and interaction through mimicry but did not create anything approaching human equivalent intelligence. Unsurprisingly AI development stagnated after these initial attempts.

The father of AI is rightly credited to be Marvin Minsky, an American cognitive research scientist who developed the first randomly wired neural network learning machine, SNARC[4] in January 1952. Minsky was also author of the book *Perceptrons* (with Seymour Papert) in 1969 that became a seminal work in the field of artificial neural networks.

For the purposes of this book I am of course paraphrasing a long and complex developmental history – there are many works which espouse the historical evolution of artificial intelligence in a much greater depth but it was subsequent to the development of the Turing test that AI research bifurcated into two distinct directions. One of which centred on the earlier approach of "emulation" – namely focussing on mimicking outwardly observable intelligent behaviours; and a new approach of "simulation" – one which was based on the view that in order to achieve machine intelligence the fundamental structure and processes of neurons firing in the human nervous system had to be simulated.

As we shall see later on, both branches of research are propelling AI development through its current renaissance. There are however still limitations. Not least due to the fact that despite much scientific endeavour, we are still a very long way off from understanding precisely how the human brain functions, and for this reason, probably a long way off from

---

4   Stochastic neural analog reinforcement calculator

developing a machine with human equivalent (or greater) levels of sentience (or feeling, perception and subjective experience), combined with objective reasoning and logic – the holy grail of *Artificial General Intelligence (AGI)* or "*Strong AI*".

Inevitably, AI research and development initiatives have themselves evolved and differentiated themselves by trial and error – as some structures have shown promise, those have been refined, so now we have lines of machine learning research and applications which may in fact have very little relationship to how neuroscience currently understands the organisation and structure of the human brain (in addition of course to those that still strive to closely model real organic brain function in so far as it is understood).

Current developments

So let's now take a slightly more detailed look at what is actually happening in the field of artificial intelligence at the moment.

As I mentioned at the beginning of this chapter, we have seen a dramatic rise in the effectiveness and use of solutions based on "*Weak AI*" or "*Narrow AI*" or *Artificial Specific Intelligence (ASI)* – AI solutions that are based around a specific, narrowly defined task or application, collectively (and somewhat confusingly) falling under the umbrella term of *IA* or *Intelligent Automation*.

There are several real-world artificial intelligence applications which are driving developments in the technology:

Image processing and tagging

Image processing as it suggests requires algorithms to analyse images or to discriminate between them to get data or to perform transformations. Facial recognition is the example that immediately springs to mind in this context, however there are more prosaic examples of this, such as include identification/image tagging – as used in applications such as Facebook to apply name labels to individuals or to ascertain other data from a visual scan, such as health of an individual or location recognition for geodata. Optical Character Recognition – where algorithms learn to read handwritten text and convert documents into digital versions is another good example of this.

3D Environment processing

3D environment processing is an extension of the image processing and tagging skill – most obviously translated into the skills required by an algorithm in a robot or a "CAV" (connected and autonomous vehicle) to spatially understand its location and environment. This uses image data but also potentially radar and lidar[5] sourced spatial scanning data to process 3D geometries. Typically this technology could also be used in free roaming robot devices including pilotless drones or robots in supermarkets tasked with reviewing stock levels.

Textual Analysis

These are techniques and algorithms which extract information from or classify textual data. Textual analysis uses two distinct approaches – one based purely on pattern recognition of words and their meanings and concatenated sequences of the same, the other on grammar driven natural language processing. In terms of practical usage, these could include social media postings, tweets or emails. The technology may then be used to provide filtering (for SPAM); information extraction – for example to pull out particular pieces of data such as names and addresses or more complex "sense based" sentiment analysis – to identify the mood of the person writing (as Facebook has recently implemented in relation to postings by members who may be potentially suicidal[6]). Text analysis is also at the heart of Chatbot technology – allowing for interaction on social media, or providing for automated first line technical support.

Speech Analysis

---

[5] Lidar measures spatial distances by illuminating objects with laser light and measuring reflections with a sensor. This can then be used to create 3D scans of objects in the immediate vicinity of the CAV.

[6] See for example http://www.bbc.co.uk/news/technology-39126027 "Facebook artificial intelligence spots suicidal users", 1st March 2017

Speech processing takes equivalent skills to those used for textual documents and applies them to the spoken word. It is this area which is seeing an incredible level of investment in the creation of personal digital home assistants from the likes of Amazon (with its Echo device), Microsoft with Cortana, Google's Home device and Apple with Siri (and now the recently launched "Homepod" speaker). As with textual analysis, speech analysis has moved into a more sophisticated realm of understanding not just the words themselves, but also the manner in which they are spoken. Emotion detection tools are now playing a key part in back office call centre SLA management[7].

Data Mining

This is the process of discovering patterns or extrapolating trends from data. Data mining algorithms are used for such things as Anomaly detection – identifying for example fraudulent entries or transactions as outliers or classifying them as known types of fraud; Association rules – detecting supermarket purchasing habits by looking at a shopper's typical shopping basket; and Predictions – predicting a variable from a set of others to extrapolate for example a credit score.

Video game virtual environment processing

Video games are a multi-billion dollar entertainment industry but they are also key sandboxes for machines to interact with and learn behaviours in relation to other elements in a virtual environment, including interacting with the players themselves[8].

Machine Learning – the basic elements

At the most simplistic level, machine learning systems are no different

---

[7] See for example Deloitte's TrueVoice software enterprise product. TrueVoice applies behaviour and emotion analytics to assist in the optimal management of call centres.

[8] See for example the August 2017 edition knowledge feature of Edge Magazine – "Machine Language" which discusses new startup SpiritAI – a business that has developed an intelligent character engine for NPCs (non-player characters) in video games, thus obviating the need for thousands of pages of pre-scripted dialogue.

from conventional computer systems in that both rely on the elements of computational hardware and software to function effectively.

Whilst many modern machine learning systems exploit huge advances in computing scale and power and make use of the vast amounts of data that are available in our "big data" society, they still need what would be recognisable as a computing platform. It is the logic or software that such systems use which differs markedly from traditional computer programs directly created by human programmers which require sequential, explicit and largely linear instructions that are followed to the letter by the machine.

I have already explained that technologists developing machine learning systems have developed a variety of solutions, methodologies, models and structures to get machines to "*think*" in a narrow AI sense. In fact so many approaches have been developed, it can be difficult for the non-computer scientist to effectively decode them. To further complicate this issue, many proprietary machine learning systems employ a "mix" of adaptive learning solutions which are optimised for the particular applications at hand. We'll step through some of these models in a moment, but for the moment, and in order to provide a consistent framework for you, the reader, it is worth setting out the very basic absolutes of machine learning systems – in other words, those conceptual elements that *all* current machine learning systems use. It is important to stress that this framework applies to that subset of AI which is *machine learning* as defined at the beginning of this chapter – the terms may not be relevant to other wider or peripheral AI technologies which are generally out of scope for the purposes of this book.

At the most simplistic level It is generally established that machine learning systems are comprised of three parts: the *Model* – that is to say the way in which the system is structured and organised – in short its architecture, including the nodes, links and weights which will be applied to the data to be processed. Then there are the *Parameters* – these are the properties of the training data that are to be learned during training and finally the *Learner* –generally comprised of a *learning algorithm* – that part of the system that adjusts the model for how it processes the parameters on a *supervised, unsupervised* or *reinforcement* basis (see below under

"*Training*") and an **activation or transfer algorithm** which defines the way in which data are to be transferred between nodes within the network by forwards and or backwards propagation (see further below under "*Backpropagation*").

Algorithms

The word "*algorithm*" is often used to generalise the entire process I have described above. In many texts you might as well substitute the words for "*magic spell*". In fact, as we have seen above, an algorithm is merely a set of complex mathematical actions expressed as a formula conceptualising the model utilised by the system. Clearly machine learning algorithms are not magic spells. More prosaically, learning algorithms selectively adapt and change the model and parameters based on the data that is introduced into the machine learning system. Rather confusingly as well, it is important to note (and often misunderstood), that simply referring to a solution that is "*algorithmic*" does not necessarily imply that that solution has any degree of artificial intelligence or machine learning.

Training

All machine learning systems need to be "*trained*" (or train themselves) with a data set – a set of data points which are intended to assist the system to "understand" the relevant narrow AI task at hand and which contain the parameters I have described above. Training data sets are, as we shall see later on in this book, an incredibly significant and important feature of these systems. The nature of the training data set provided however is very different depending upon whether the system is designed to learn on a "*supervised*", "*unsupervised*" or "*reinforcement*" basis.

Supervised Learning

Supervised learning systems are provided with guiding or labelled training data sets that contain a mass of examples of the desired answers and outputs. In such cases, the training data are subsets of data that are well known in terms of all of their features, content, correlations and so forth and thus can provide a good representative example to benchmark the outputs of the system. Typically these data sets will be past, real life examples of the problem the system has been configured to resolve. Usually this type of machine learning supports evaluation, classification or prediction outcomes.

Unsupervised Learning

Systems that are designed to learn on an unsupervised basis in contrast are provided with unlabelled data that may or may not contain the desired answer or output. In these cases, the systems attempt to find either outliers or correlations or patterns in the data without any form of guidance. Provided data sets may be clustered into different classes that share some common characteristics – unsurprisingly, this is often referred to as "*clustering*" by the industry. Typically, this type of machine learning is found in forensic tools.

Reinforcement Learning

Reinforcement learning is a similar process to unsupervised learning – however machine learning systems here are typically exposed to a rules-based competitive environment where they train themselves continuously using trial and error to try to find the best reward – which might be winning a game or earning more money. This type of AI system attempts to learn from past experience in order to refine and improve decision outcomes, and is particularly well suited to closed environments with a static framework.

Whether the system is designed to work on a supervised or unsupervised basis it is clearly vitally important that the data sets provided to train the system need to be representative of the underlying problem the system is being designed to resolve and should not be unbalanced or skewed in any particular direction. As we'll see later on in this book, there are particular issues with this which could trap the unwary. Proactively editing out bias too far in a data set may well have the opposite and undesired effect of making that data set too specific (so called "*overfitting*") and less representative of the data class, in turn leading to the corresponding outputs of the system being prejudiced in favour of or against particular outcomes.

Backpropagation

Backpropagation is the process which allows a machine learning system to adjust and change by reference to previous outcomes. In technical terms it is the means by which the machine learning system (via the *activation algorithm*, see above) computes and optimises the gradient descent required in the calculation of weights used in the network by distributing *back* through network nodes.

So these are the basic features of AI or machine learning systems. As I mentioned above, there are a variety of different AI *Models* which are being deployed, and it is worth spending a little time on the most significant of these.

Artificial Neural Networks

Artificial neural networks aim to most closely model the functioning of the human brain through the simulation approach and contain all of the basic machine learning elements described above.

Neuroscience has established that the human neo-cortex, which is where most of our higher brain function resides, consists of a very dense population of interconnected neurons or brain cells. Neurons consist of the soma (the cell body) and axons and dendrites (the filaments that extend from the cell itself). Observed higher human brain functions require groups or networks of neurons to fire together in electro chemical activity. Even though the base physical structure of the cortex is the same, it is settled science that there are cortical regions that specialise in particular skills, such as language, motor movement, sight and hearing. More recently, it has been established that there are progressively "higher" levels of brain processing driven by layers of neurons. You might for example have a collection of neurons at a low level that are specialised in the visual detection of "edges". Data from these lower functions is passed up the tree (or network) to higher functions, such as those that might detect nose shapes or eye shapes, so that collectively, you are able to perceive a face[9].

In the world of artificial intelligence, scientists have attempted to replicate or model these structures and their functionality by use of neural networks. In simplistic terms, neural networks can be organised as "shallow" – 1-3 layers or "deep" – over 7 layers (as is generally the case in the human neo-cortex).

Artificial neural networks are composed of artificial input "neurons" – virtual computing "cells" that *activate*, that is to say, assume a numeric value (by reference to a chosen algorithm which applies weights and biases to that numeric value – in effect influencing it) and then hand it off to another layer of the network, which also applies an algorithmic treatment to it, and so on and so forth until the data has passed through the entire network and is outputted.

The process is heavily mathematical. Most neural networks apply something called a *cost function*, which is an additional mathematical process that determines how to adjust the network's weights and biases in order to make it more accurate. Typically this is achieved by something called *gradient descent* – a calculus derived mathematical function which is designed to reach the *minima* (the lowest possible, and hence the most accurate value, of the *cost function* described above).

Stepping away from the maths for a moment, it is worth making the point that Artificial Neural Networks process data in a non-linear manner – as we saw from the basic elements section above, data may *backpropagate* as well as move forwards through the network (a further mathematically driven process of output refinement and tuning). They are often therefore referred to as "*black boxes*". This can make it very difficult to understand and equally difficult to explain how or why the system has reached a particular outcome in a particular instance.

It is also important to note that neural networks come in a variety of flavours, so for example ***Regression Neural Networks*** are neural networks

---

9 Bizarrely, scientist have apparently discovered that there is a neuron that appears to be dedicated to Bill Clinton recognition. See *On Intelligence*, by Jeff Hawkins.

that are trained to analyse data on either a linear or non-linear regression basis (a simple example of regression analysis might be extrapolating growth rates from height measurements taken from a child).

Convolutional Neural Networks or ("*CNNs*") have a structure which is specifically optimised for image recognition (such networks assume that all inputs are image related). *Generative Adversarial Networks* ("*GANs*") take this one step further and improve applications such as image recognition and optimisation by pitting one CNN against another. One network acts as image generator, the other acts as image discriminator, challenging the generating network to improve. Use of this technique has proved very valuable in picture enhancement – such as for example improving the resolution of fuzzy images or removing artefacts.

GANs are also particularly effective where no correlated data exists to underpin decisions relating to a processing application – in other words, they can be used to synthesise data where none actually exist. One particular company for example uses such an approach to synthesise claims data for insurers to enable them to more accurately model and price risk for the underwriting process[10].

Deep Learning Networks

Deep learning models are simply varieties of artificial neural networks that employ vastly greater computing power, more recent algorithmic innovations and much bigger data sets – in short, they take advantage of the much greater computing power available to us, but operate in much the same manner as I have described above. Of course, the challenges of explainability and transparency are also correspondingly amplified when such networks are used.

On a wider basis, it is probably worth providing a brief introduction to some other non-machine learning AI technologies, although I do not propose to delve into these in any great detail.

---

[10] Cytora's Risk Engine product – see www.cytora.com

Decision Trees

In contrast to machine learning, decision trees are a *"white box"* artificial intelligence model – typically their decisions are more easily explicable and they are principally used for classification style problems. In simple terms a decision tree works by processing data through a series of question "nodes" (similar to a flow diagram type structure). Each node hands off data to corresponding next layer once a question has been answered. Decision trees usually work on a Boolean basis (ie *yes* or *no*).

Decision trees depend upon being able to classify data sets in an expected manner and are not suitable for applications that are based on unsupervised pattern correlation or recognition. This means that they are in turn susceptible to in-built bias if the overall problem they are designed to resolve has been incorrectly modelled.

Random Forests

Random Forests and Deep Forests are very large ensembles of Decision Trees. In simple terms, Random Forests take random subsets of data to be analysed and assign these to individual trees. The collective output of the trees provides a range of responses which can be correlated on a statistical basis to provide a stronger prediction than a single decision tree alone. I do not propose to explain the intricacies of these structures further in this book, however the reader should note that by aggregating decision trees together in a very large hierarchy, such structures may become inherently less explicable in terms of their decision making.

Probabilistic artificial intelligence

Probabilistic or Bayesian artificial intelligence techniques are some of the hardest to conceptualise and understand. They may or may not incorporate machine learning technology. Systems that work on this basis are attempting, by application of mathematical probability theory, to express all forms of uncertainty associated with the problem the model is trying to resolve. They then apply inverse probability (***Bayes' Rule***) to infer unknown characteristics of the problem to make predictions about, and learn from observed data (so called "*inference algorithms*").

The greatest strength of Probabilistic models is that they *know what they do not know* or in effect have an internal representation of past outcomes that are learned, on the basis of which they can guess a probable outcome. We live and work in a very messy world – and many decisions we take are inferred from observable data sets that are incomplete. Such systems are therefore incredibly powerful but do depend on a very careful probabilistic representation of uncertainty.

So that was an introduction to the key elements of the technology. In so far as political, regulatory and industry responses are concerned, there are a number that are worth mentioning, as they reflect well some of the issues and concerns raised in this book.

Naturally since the last edition of this work, these responses have multiplied in number and complexity to the extent that they have now been accorded their own separate chapter. In this regard I would direct you to Chapter twelve.

CHAPTER TWO
CAUSATION AND ARTIFICIAL INTELLIGENCE

AI Liability: A Sliding Scale

Liability is essentially a scalable concept which is based factually on the degree of legal responsibility society places on a *person*. As we will see later on, historically responsibility and hence liability levels are not static – the able-minded, children and mentally incapable adults all have different levels of liability – the latter having little or no responsibility for their actions and therefore a commensurately lower level of accountability and liability.

The degree to which an artificially intelligent system could in theory assume responsibility for its actions thus depends, from a philosophical perspective (and taking aside any need to amend the law to account for such liability), on the extent to which it is aware of those actions. In the previous chapter, we saw that the current state of the art is providing us with some very clever discrete (or narrow) solutions to particular problems. This does not yet equate however to human levels of sentience or even self-awareness.

Until relatively recently, the question of whether or not a machine should be accountable and hence liable for its actions was a relatively trite one – a machine was merely a tool of the person using or operating it. There was absolutely no question of machines assuming a level of personal accountability or even "*personhood*" as they were incapable of autonomous or semi-autonomous action. This is essentially the way in which the law has evolved to deal with machine generated consequences.

We are now however poised to deal with how to creatively twist our liability frameworks so as to account for the consequences created by autonomous machine action. Before we get into a discussion of existing liability frameworks, it is worth exploring this sliding scale theme. With this in mind, future liability frameworks are going to need to differentiate between traditional "dumb" machines at the one end, and super-intelligent semi or fully sentient machines at the other end.

A "*HAL 9000*" sentient supercomputer will have a greater degree of autonomy, independent thought and hence greater consequences coming from its action, and when it is created is very likely to be imbued with some form of personhood. In a sense, the two ends of the spectrum are easy to rationalise – the real conundrum is dealing with the liability consequences of a machine sandwiched between the HAL 9000 and the toaster: one which has properties of independent and autonomous action but not the clear attributes of a person as we understand it.

Complexity – A causative blocker

Taking aside the degree to which an AI system can assume awareness for its actions, there is a rather more immediate problem in the usage of current AI systems which is driven by the legal concept of *causation*. We will look at existing liability frameworks shortly, but put simply, in order to establish liability you need to demonstrate that the person or thing *caused* the relevant loss or damage.

Existing causative liability models work well when machine functions (and hence responses) can by and large be traced back to human design, programming and knowledge.

In machine learning systems this is usually very difficult to achieve especially in artificial neural networks or probabilistic Bayesian networks where computer scientists are often unable to determine how or why (on a human explicable basis) a machine learning system has made a particular decision.

The current "*state of the art*" does not provide for systems to self-report their decisions, but there is a widely held view in the relevant scientific community that regulators will force developers to interject "explanation systems" into their AI solutions where they are deployed in environments where their outputs (or decisions) are likely to have a significant regulatory or human impact such as healthcare or financial services[11].

There are technical concerns however that these explanation systems may impair or limit the operation of the core machine learning system (by constraining them to a narrower spectrum of decisions that are human explicable) and may be of limited use where the rationale or decision adopted by the ML system is not capable of human explanation. As noted earlier, probabilistic Bayesian networks and artificial neural networks are particularly difficult to decipher owing to their structures – decision trees may be slightly easier (decision tree networks that are organised into Random Forests may however regain *"black box"* characteristics).

Interestingly, there is a current theoretical view that distributive, decentralised blockchain technology may provide the ideal characteristics for an auditable framework for such explanation systems by underpinning and logging in an immutable way each step of the artificial reasoning process – however we are some distance from any such auditing technology being introduced in practical terms.

Aside from the question of whether a decision is traceable from a causative viewpoint, it may also be incorrect to classify an undesired decision or "learned behaviour" adopted by a machine learning system as subjectively wrong – just because a system produces an undesirable result does not mean it is defective.

AI systems are renowned for what are known as their *"edge case"* decisions – those decisions which are at the margins of the probability curve for their operating parameters. Much scientific effort is devoted to tuning out these edge cases, but they still occur (indeed in some cases these outcomes may be positively encouraged).

---

[11] See Chapter twelve for a discussion on the EU's White Paper on Artificial Intelligence. Mandating that AI demonstrates a level of explainability commensurate with the harm it may cause is a direction of travel that the EU appears to be moving in.

Counterfactual Analysis

Finally, on the issue of explicability and machine learning, it is worth briefly mentioning the concept of counterfactuals as a mathematical response. What a counterfactual aims to do is essentially provide a rationale for a given circumstance by positing what might have happened had the given circumstance *not* actually occurred – for example *had I not stepped onto the ice, I wouldn't have slipped.*

In machine learning, counterfactual analysis can be used to explain how a machine learning model got to a particular prediction, which is a particularly useful technique given the opaque nature of many of these systems.

In machine learning, the prediction itself is the outcome, and the particular parameters or "feature values" which were input into the model are the causes of that outcome. Changing these feature values cause the prediction to change but not necessarily in a way which reflects the real causal relationships of the data in the machine learning model. Hence you can arrive at a plausible "cause" without actually understanding the real reason the model predicted in the way that it did. Of course, whilst valuable, counterfactuals can introduce an additional problem of multiple truths – or the so-called Rashomon effect[12], itself mitigated by evaluating all counterfactual explanations in any given instance and prioritising them for suitability and likelihood.

Existing liability frameworks

So, with this in mind, let's review the existing liability frameworks which could conceivably apply to what are termed "*machine generated consequences*". Current liability frameworks are focussed on product liability generally – broken down into three distinct categories: Contract law, Negligence (tort) and, so far as the UK (and EU) is concerned, strict liability under consumer protection legislation (in the UK the Consumer

---

[12] This was named after the Japanese movie "Rashomon" which features the murder of a Samurai and the multiple, contradicting but highly plausible explanations for his murder provided by several witnesses.

Protection Act 1987).

We'll review the scope of each briefly in a moment and then consider potential issues in relation to their application to AI systems. In this context, the most conventional analysis we can apply to intelligent or semi-intelligent machines is as complex products.

Using the driverless car as an example, what we can see is that in fact it is an assemblage of many and varied integrated systems that are produced by multiple manufacturers. For a driverless car to work effectively, it needs sensors to navigate road obstructions, such as radar and lidar detection. It must have a computer to direct its actions and that computer needs to have a logic framework within which to operate – internally by use of its own operating software and also externally by reference to map data. All of these systems need to work together effectively, and this is without consideration of all the usual mechanical components which form a standard car, which must also be present and functioning.

Taking aside the organisational complexity of the AI system itself which we have already discussed, this mechanical complexity alone gives rise to a potential plethora of liability targets, ranging from the vehicle manufacturer itself, all the way down to the designer of an individual component, depending upon where the actual defect, fault or breach occurs.

Contract

Contract clearly has a role to play in determining product-based liability. Contracts ensure that manufacturers and retailers sell products that meet agreed pre-determined standards. Such liability is obviously aimed at the recovery of financial (or pure economic) loss as a result of breach of these contractual standards, however obviously, as we are all aware, contract liability can in some circumstances lead to the recovery of damages for consequential loss.

Contract terms and hence liability may be either express – as to defects and warranties or implied. In the UK there are implied terms as to quality, fitness for purpose, title and description in the Consumer Rights Act 2015 so far as B2C contracts are concerned and the Sale of Goods Act 1979 for B2B contracts. Although there is not a focus on *"defects"* per se under the Sale of Goods legislation, there is clearly an emphasis on conformity with description. Arguably that could amount to nearly the same thing: a failure to conform to a description or specification is very close to a "*defect*" in practical terms.

We'll take a look at the relevant strengths and weaknesses of contract liability in this context in a moment, but it is worth remembering that contract is a *causative* based liability framework. In order to found liability, the Claimant must prove that there was a breach of either an express or an implied term and that that breach caused the loss. Contract causation is often overlooked as the poor cousin of tort causation but ever since the time of *Hadley v. Baxendale*[13], it is still a relevant factor in determining liability. This is an important consideration – and again one we'll return to later.

Finally, it is worth remembering that the primary remedy for breach of contract is damages (as assessed to put the innocent party in the position they would have been had the contract been correctly performed). The primary advantage of contract liability is of course that it is open to the contract counterparties to determine the scope of the contract responsibilities and obligations as between them and hence the liability if things do go wrong. This means that it is quite open to tailor the agreement to the functions and performance of the AI system involved.

So far as the implied terms are concerned, Section 9 of the Consumer Rights Act provides that where goods are sold "in the course of a business" there is an implied term that the goods are of *satisfactory quality*[14] and *fit for a purpose*[15] that the buyer has made known to the seller. Products are therefore of satisfactory quality if they meet the standard that a reasonable person would regard as satisfactory, taking into account their description, price and all other relevant circumstances. In other words it

---

[13] [1854] EWHC J70

[14] s9

[15] s10

could be argued that contract implied terms create a consumer expectation test.

The major disadvantage of contract liability of course is that it is not a liability that applies generally to the "whole world" but rather is one which is constrained by *contract privity* (albeit with limited exceptions in some jurisdictions – such as the Contract (Rights of Third Parties) Act 1999 in the UK).

This means that obligations can only be enforced by contract counterparties. Of course – in some situations it is possible to conceive of a contract relationship subsisting in your use of an intelligent systems – but equally speaking in many others, there will not be. Aside from this, there is a lack of consistency in contractual standards in relation to contracts for the sale of goods which make the application of the framework complex. So, for example, for public policy reasons there are higher standards which apply to contracts made with consumers – the Consumer Rights Act requires that in assessing whether products are of satisfactory quality that account is taken of any *"public statements on the specific characteristics of the goods made about them by the Seller or the producer, particularly in advertising"*[16].

Tort

Product liability in tort refers to a breach of a duty of care in negligence. Since the seminal case of *Donoghue v. Stevenson*[17], tortious duties can run concurrently with contractual liabilities. The essence of the case was that if a consumer purchases products in a form intended to reach him or her without the possibility of reasonable intermediate examination and with the knowledge on the part of the producer that the absence of reasonable care in the preparation of the product will result in personal injury or property damage, which is reasonably foreseeable, then that producer owes a duty to take reasonable care in their production. *Donoghue v. Stevenson* concerned decomposed snails in ginger beer bottles but it does not

---

[16] s9(5)

[17] [1932] AC 562

take much to extrapolate that analysis to a driverless car or a surgical ro-bot.

Again, it is worth pointing out the causative nature of tort as a liability framework – it is essentially fault based. The claimant must prove that the defendant owed him or her a duty of care, they failed in that standard and damage was caused as a result.

In contrast to contractual damages, tort-based damages are awarded on the basis of putting the injured party in the position they would have been had the tort not occurred. The scope of potential liability in tort is wide. It could equally apply to manufacturers, producers and anyone di-rectly involved in the manufacture and distribution of a product with a defect. You do however need to establish that a duty of care subsists and was breached – and irrespective of this that the relevant chain of causation is not broken by the damage being too remote.

There are a number of disadvantages with this liability framework – and it is worth pointing them out briefly. There are very real difficulties in claiming damages for pure economic loss in tort – certainly so far as the UK is concerned, and since the high watermark of *Junior Books v. Ve-itchi*[18], there are only a limited number of circumstances where this is possible, including for example, negligent advice from surveyors.

Contributory negligence can also act as a defence to liability, if it is shown that the claimant should have known of the defect but negligently failed to recognise it or negligently used the product or failed to take account of its operating instructions. In such cases damages are reduced to a de-gree which is commensurate with the claimant's negligence.

Volenti non fit injuria – or voluntary assumption of risk is less common in product liability cases – on the basis that if a claimant knows of the defect they are less likely to use it and if they do, that usually breaks the causative chain between defect and damage.

---

[18] [1983] 1 AC 520

As we have seen, as intelligent machines and AI systems "learn" for themselves, their behaviours are increasingly less and less directly attributable to human programming. These machines are not acting on a prescriptive instruction set, but a system of rules that may not have anticipated the precise circumstances under which the machine should act. To take our prior example of the autonomous vehicle, what if our car has been programmed to look after and preserve the safety of its occupants and also to avoid pedestrians at all costs and is placed in an unavoidable situation where it has to make a decision as to whether to avoid a pedestrian crossing into its path (and thereby run into a brick wall, injuring or even killing its occupants) or running over the pedestrian (and thereby saving its occupants). Can any outcome of that decision be said to be a failure or a defect – even if people are injured or possibly killed as a result?[19]

In tort, the doctrine of *res ipsa loquitur* – or the thing speaks for itself assists in providing a partial solution to the problem. The doctrine is equally applicable in the US and the UK.

Res ipsa loquitur is useful in dealing with cases where there are multiple successive inexplicable failures which cannot in themselves be readily explained. A classic example of the application of this was in the US case of *Toyota Motor Corporation*[20], where Toyota found that for no particular reason, many of its high-end Lexus model cars simply accelerated – despite the intervention of their drivers. After extensive investigation, the cause of these failures could not be pinpointed by the manufacturer. Toyota took the step of settling 400 pending case against it after a jury applied the doctrine *of res ipsa loquitur* and awarded the plaintiffs in that case $3m in damages.

In the UK the principles are enshrined in the leading case of *Scott and*

---

[19] This is the so-called "trolley car" problem postulated by Philippa Foot in "*The Problem of Abortion and the Doctrine of the Double Effect*" Oxford Review, Number 5, 1967

[20] See *In re Toyota Motor Corp. unintended acceleration marketing, sales practices and products liability litigation*, 978 F.Supp.2d 1053 (C.D.Cal. 2013), 92 Fed. R. Evid. Serv. 714, Prod.Liab.Rep. (CCH) P 19, 244, 2013 WL 5763178

Bennett v Chemical Construction (GB) Ltd[21]. This provides for a three-step test for the principle to be applied: (i) the event or accident would not ordinarily have occurred in the absence of negligence (ii) the thing causing the damage must be under the control of the defendant and (iii) there is no evidence as to the cause of the event or accident. Clearly such a test will need to be considered in the context of artificially intelligent machines and the extent to which such a device can be considered to be "under the control" of its user when it is making decisions on its own behalf will be debateable to a greater or lesser degree. What this doctrine also does not provide a solution to of course is the inexplicable *isolated* incident.

Finally, it should be emphasised that on a factual basis, proving liability in tort can be very difficult – especially in product liability cases, as very often the details that are required to show liability are held by the defendant. Obviously there are mechanisms in litigation to get hold of that information – but typically a defendant will not go out of the way to disclose it and might use any number of established disclosure tricks to bury the key facts or at least make them very difficult to ascertain.

Strict Liability: Consumer Protection

The Consumer Protection Act 1987 ("CPA") implements the EU directive on Liability for Defective Products[22]. This Act introduces a strict liability regime which does not affect the general availability of Contract and Tort based remedies. What the Act provides is that a person who is injured or whose personal property is damaged by a product will be able to claim against a manufacturer or supplier of that product (and certain other third parties) if it can be shown that the product was defective.

There is no requirement to prove fault on the part of the manufacturer but obviously there is a requirement on the claimant to show that the defect existed on the preponderance of the evidence. The Act introduces a consumer expectations test in that a defect exists where "*the safety of the*

---

[21] [1971] 3 All ER 822

[22] 85/374/EC

product is not such as persons generally are entitled to expect[23]. Consumer expectations themselves are subject to a reasonableness test.

In terms of the advantages of the CPA regime – as previously discussed – there is no requirement to show fault; neither is there a privity requirement – the regime itself allows for a wide variety of potential liability targets, including suppliers and manufacturers.

There are still some problems with consumer protection product liability however – obviously causation still exists – although it is limited to the finding of defects and moderated by a consumer expectation test. Furthermore, the Act is designed to cover claims for real damage, so does not encompass claims for pure economic loss.

In the context of artificial intelligence, there are also problems with the definition of "*Product*" under the Act. Product is defined as "*any goods or electricity and includes products aggregated into other products, whether as component parts, raw materials or otherwise*"[24]. Quite ambiguously for our purposes the Act is not clear as to whether software and/or other products of an intellectual type are included in the definition of its scope. Disembodied software per se is typically not treated as a "good" under English law although there is an argument which might encompass software embedded into functional hardware. Anecdotally, the Consumer Rights Act may also provide some correlative instruction so far as Sale of Goods legislation is concerned in its Chapter 3, which explicitly provides that the supply of digital content should be treated neither as goods nor as a service but as a separate class of supply[25]. Chapter nine of this book (Sector Specific Considerations) looks at the implications of Chapter 3 of the CRA in a little more detail.

Finally, there is also the "*developmental risks defence*", which provides a defence to the manufacturer "*if the scientific and technical knowledge at the time the product was manufactured was not such that a producer of a*

---

[23] s3(1)

[24] s1(2)(c)

[25] s33 et seq

similar product might have been able to discover the defect"[26]. This is obviously highly relevant to our current discussion – products including machine learning and artificial intelligence will inevitably involve the "state of the art" in relation to their development.

Future Liability Frameworks

Insurance

There are clear public policy arguments now for the introduction of a strict liability insurance-based model for artificially intelligent systems. The 1973 Accident Compensation Act in New Zealand is a classic example of such a system working in practice – it applies generally to compensation for all accidents. In New Zealand, accidents are not litigated, but rather victim compensation is automatically paid at Government set tariffs and funded by insurance premiums.

Negligence and breach of contract actions are becoming more and more complex to litigate – as resources are spent identifying what has (or indeed might) have gone wrong. In particular, the argument runs that from a social justice perspective, it is better spending the money compensating the victims of accidents and incidents involving autonomous systems than it is on expensive lawyers and expert witnesses.

So far as research and development is concerned, a strict liability insurance-based model would also incentivise research on new intelligent AI based systems, rather than forcing R&D divisions of corporations to consider what defensive steps they should be taking to avoid a class action.

What has the UK been doing to address this challenge? We've seen the most movement in the CAV space.

The UK Government recently enacted the Automated and Electric Vehicles Act 2018 (the AEVA 2018). Rather than go down the strict liability route I mentioned earlier, the UK has chosen to address the issue of driverless cars from the perspective of gaps in current insurance coverage

---

[26] s4(1)e

caused by fully autonomous driving.

Section 2(1) of the AEVA 2018 provides that *"where…an accident is caused by an automated vehicle when driving itself…the vehicle is insured at the time of the accident, and…an insured person or any other person suffers damage as a result of the accident, the insurer is liable for that damage."*

In essence the principle enshrined in the Act is that if you are hit by an insured party's vehicle that is self-driving at the time, the insurer "at fault" pays out. If you have comprehensive cover then you will also be insured for your own injuries. If the vehicle at fault is not covered by insurance then the Motor Insurers Bureau will pay out in the usual way and seek to recover its losses from the owner of the uninsured vehicle.

This is an essentially pragmatic response that will probably work in an environment where there is a mixed demographic of driverless cars and human piloted ones – it also avoids systemic change to the insurance industry. It does however completely sidestep the causation issues described earlier in this chapter.

Crucially, the measure relies very heavily on the ability of insurers to subrogate and therefore bring claims of their own against other third parties, including manufacturers. This will of course be hugely problematic for insurers if the relevant fault or defect cannot easily be traced.

Turing Registries

Some commentators[27] have argued specifically that for intelligent machines we need to go a step further and set up what have been termed "Turing Registries" after the great computer pioneer Alan Turing.

This would work by submitting intelligent machines to a testing and certification process to quantify the certification based on a spectrum as follows: the higher the intelligence and autonomy and hence greater conse-

---

[27] See for example *"Liability for Distributed Artificial Intelligences"*, Curtis E.A. Karnow, Berkeley Technology Law Journal 1996, Vol 11.1, page 147

quences for failure, the higher the premium payable to "release" that machine into the working environment. The premium payable for certification would be paid by the developer or manufacturer of the AI entity wanting to deploy the AI into the market. Much as in the manner of the New Zealand strict liability insurance model discussed earlier, the premiums would fund a "common pool" under which risks would be paid out. The system could become self-fulfilling if AIs were prohibited from use without this certification.

As has been pointed out, this model is similar, but *not identical* to insurance – it does remove causation and proximate cause but also allows for the wilful acts of AIs – normally something that is excluded by insurance.

The EU's likely direction of travel

Many of the issues discussed in this chapter remain open for debate within the EU, although, as you will see below and in Chapter twelve, there are moves there to impose a new liability regime for artificially intelligent systems[28], following the introduction of the EU White Paper on Artificial Intelligence.

The EU's White Paper alludes to an earlier research paper on Liability by the New Technologies formation (NTF) of the High Level Expert Group (HLEG) on AI[29]. Whilst this paper does not in any sense represent official EU policy on AI, it is useful to review some of its key findings as these may form the basis of a nascent EU liability framework. Indeed, there are some indirect hints that the contents of this HLEG paper generally inform thinking behind the the official EU White Paper is influenced and informed by its contents.

---

[28] See Chapter twelve more generally and also: White Paper on Artificial Intelligence – A European approach to excellence and trust COM (2020) 65 final, 19.2.2020 available at https://ec.europa.eu/info/sites/info/files/commission-white-paper-artificial-intelligence-feb2020_en.pdf

[29] *Liability for Artificial Intelligence and other emerging digital technologies* – https://ec.europa.eu/transparency/regexpert/index.cfm?do=groupDetail.group-MeetingDoc&docid=36608

The overarching conclusion of the HLEG paper was that digital technologies fundamentally affect the way in which we interact with society and that this has an inevitable impact on liability law.

Specifically, the features of digital technology such as complexity, opacity, interconnectedness, autonomy, lack of predictability, (amongst others) are all features which impact liability and could cause harm. The view was that these features did not fit well with current (traditional) liability laws and could cause imbalances in the efficient allocation of loss (because e.g. the accountable party cannot be identified). With the above in mind, specific recommendations included the following:

Operator strict liability

The HLEG paper concluded that strict liability was deemed to be an appropriate response to risks posed by digital technologies – if such use may cause significant harm. The principle proposed here was that strict liability should lie with the person who was in control of the risk connected with the operation of the technology. If however there were two or more operators (for example the user or "front end" operator and a person providing back end support) then strict liability should lie with the party who had more control over the risks of operation.

Producer strict liability

Significantly, the HLEG considered that producers should play a key role in indemnifying damage caused by defective products and their components – irrespective of whether they took a digital or tangible form (this is significant because current product liability regimes tend to exclude software and other intangible products).

The HLEG considered that producers should be strictly liable for defects in digital technologies even if defects appeared after the product was put into circulation, and proposed the disapplication of the so-called "Developmental risks defence".

Fault liability and duties of care

Here it was proposed that operators of digital technologies should have to comply with adapted duties of care in relation to choosing the right system; monitoring the system and maintaining it. Correspondingly, producers should have to design, describe and market products in a way which enabled operators to comply with these adapted duties. It was also thought that producers should in addition adequately monitor their product after putting it in to circulation.

Logging by design

Again, somewhat controversially, a new concept of *"Logging by Design"* was proposed, which has clear echoes of *"Privacy by Design"* in a GDPR context. Here, the HLEG considered that there should be a duty on producers to equip technology with a means of recording information about its operation (essentially mandating the "decoding" of decisions made by opaque black box systems) – if such information was essential for establishing whether or not a particular risk had materialised.

We have already seen that in many cases the ability to determine how or why a black box system reached a particular conclusion is either not technologically possible or is currently an imprecise science. Clearly this obligation is aspirational, and admirable in its intent, but potentially at odds with the way in which deep neural networks actually work.

Significantly, what the HLEG said was that the absence of this logging capability should give the victim a rebuttable presumption of proof of liability.

Burden of proving causation

As a general rule, the HLEG concluded that victims should continue to be required to prove what caused the relevant harm. Where the "challenges" of the technology made this harder however, the burden of proof could be "alleviated" in a similar manner to the principle of *res ipsa loquitur* (see earlier in this Chapter).

Burden of proving fault

In another somewhat controversial conclusion, the HLEG considered that the burden of proving fault should be reversed if, given the circumstances of the particular case, there were *disproportionate difficulties*[30] and the costs of establishing the relevant standard of care justified it.

Insurance and Compensation funds

In its last recommendation, with a nod to the concept of Turing Registries discussed earlier, the HLEG proposed that some form of mandatory insurance might be more appropriate in cases where the risk of harm was more frequent and the operator was less able to indemnify the victim. In this vein it was argued that compensation funds should be established to protect victims whose claims could not be satisfied (in much the same way as the motor insurance directive provides for funds for victims of uninsured motor accidents).

Individuation or Artificial Personhood

The last topic in this Chapter that we touch upon is a brief discussion of *artificial personhood* as this is a liability concept that has ignited much debate.

We have already hopefully dispelled the myth that AGI or artificial general intelligence is a close prospect. It is however worth considering briefly the inevitable question of how our liability rules will cope with machines if at some stage they do *individuate* – or develop distinct legal personalities and individual identities of their own. Clearly if machines possess a human equivalent personality of their own then there is no reason why

---

[30] The HLEG does not explain what these disproportionate difficulties might be in any detail. Instead the report states *"Features of emerging digital technologies such as opacity, openness, autonomy and limited predictability may often result in unreasonable difficulties or costs for the plaintiff to prove facts necessary for the establishment of fault. At the same time, the proof of relevant facts may be much easier for the defendant (producer or operator of the technology). This asymmetry justifies the reversal of the burden of proof."* See page 55

they cannot directly accrue liability through the concept of *"artificial personhood"* in the same manner in which living breathing humans accrue it. The European Parliament considered this question in a recommendation on granting robots and AI's legal status to the Commission on *Civil Law Rules on Robotics*[31]. Part of their recommended approach was to propose a registration system for intelligent robots in much the same manner as the Turing Registries we describe above. The recommendation on special legal personality was recently ultimately criticised in an open letter to the Commission signed by over 150 AI and robotics specialists. This was followed up by the HLEG paper we discussed earlier in this chapter[32] which has made it clear that legal personality is an effective "dead end" for causation purposes on the basis that most harm can be reducible to risks attributed to natural persons or existing categories of legal persons.

For the more distant future, there are no answers here obviously, but rather questions. We can however consider some current and historical legal analogues. How are we going to treat self-aware machines and are we going to fall into the unfortunate historical bear traps of the past? The historical treatment of slaves bears particular scrutiny in this regard and the questions raised by that treatment are no less relevant now, although not for discussion in this book.

If we walk further down the path of individuation, and give them personal liability, how are we going to apply legal duties of care to intelligent machines?

Obviously the law already recognises circumstances where there is a reduced level of legal liability owing to a commensurately reduced ability to distinguish right from wrong – the principle of *Doli Incapax* in relation to infants and the mentally incapable spring to mind in this regard. Might some machines that are not fully capable of understanding the consequences of their actions fall within this principle in the future?

---

[31] 27th January 2017 2015/2103 (INL), see in particular paragraph 59 f.

[32] Liability for Artificial Intelligence and other emerging digital technologies – see note 20 for hypertext link

We are now effectively at a "*tipping point*" in how we manage the machine generated consequences of our new AI creations. As we have seen, Contract, Tort and Strict Liability consumer protection laws are effective to a degree in relation to managing these consequences but effectively break down where cause and effect cannot be made out.

CHAPTER THREE
BIG DATA AND ARTIFICIAL INTELLIGENCE

It is of course, big data that sits at the heart of artificial intelligence.

As computing systems generally have grown in power and capacity, so the consumption of data has grown exponentially. One of the most exciting developments of machine learning is its ability to analyse data in vastly more dimensions than human beings have ever been able to, at a far quicker pace. This ability to spot unexpected correlations and patterns in data is incredibly powerful and has already provided some very surprising applications – one US insurance start up[33] for example can analyse a "selfie" using thousands of different facial data points to determine how quickly an individual is ageing, their gender, body mass index and whether they smoke. Their system predicts life expectancy of individuals much more accurately than traditional methods. Another system developed by researchers at Stanford University can apparently (and somewhat controversially) identify an individual's sexuality by identifying or correlating a complex series of facial characteristics[34]. Even more outlandishly, there is a machine learning system it is claimed can reconstruct a reasonable facsimile of someone's face from the sound of their voice[35].

Not unsurprisingly, the potential for such AI solutions to have a significant impact on personal life and privacy has drawn the attention of legislators and is a feature of the new General Data Protection Regulation (or "GDPR") which we'll look at shortly. Before we do this however, and in order to provide a framework for our analysis, it is worth describing

---

[33] Lapetus Solutions Inc.

[34] https://osf.io/zn79k/ "Deep Neural Networks are more accurate than humans in detecting sexual orientation from facial images", Wang, Kosinski, 2017

[35] This is *Speech2Face*, a deep neural network created by MIT researchers. See https://www.onartificialintelligence.com/articles/17429/ai-generates-human-faces-based-on-their-voices

how machine learning systems acquire and generate data and typically how they process such data.

It should also be pointed out that the data acquisition and manipulation features of AI systems are not unique to this technology but are amplified to an extreme degree by machine learning. Analytics are very much a product of the complex data producing society that we now live in.

For the most part we tend to think of the handing over of data (including personal data) to third parties as a conscious transaction which we positively have to provide our pro-active consent for. In fact, this is an outmoded view of reality. In many cases now, data (some of which will inevitably be "personal") is generated automatically by the variety of "smart" devices we interact with. Indeed, we don't even need to actively interact with a device for data to be generated about us. We could be the subjects of a facial recognition system at an airport or have our mobile phones queried by MAC and other network "sniffers" without even being aware of it. Indeed, this is one of the ways COVID-19 *"Track and Trace"* apps function. Your phone acts as a geolocator and identifies whether or not you have been in close contact with an infected person.

Predictive Analytics

The Information Accountability Foundation (IAF) has identified four types of data that form the basis of data analytics[36] – that is to say multiple items of data which in broad terms together disclose a *pattern* (ie typically of usage or consumption in terms of a particular device or movement in terms of surveillance etc.). These types of data are *"Provided"* data (as described above) the most traditional means – that data that is consciously given by individuals. *"Observed"* data might be data drawn from surveillance systems. *"Derived"* data is data drawn directly from other sources to produce new classes of data, and *"Inferred"* data is produced typically by analysis of existing data to make predictions. It is this last class of data which are referred to as predictive data analytics (or more simply *predictive analytics*) where machine learning systems have been

---

[36] "The origins of personal data and its implications for governance", OECD March 2014

making ever impressive technological advances.

The most immediate influence of this is best illustrated by the systemic impact predictive analytics are having on the insurance industry, which has been quick to embrace their potential. Quite apart from the jobs impact in relation to claims handling and processing, the technology is transforming the way in which insurance companies model risk and hence price premiums.

At its most simple level, insurers model risk by way of a concept known as "*pooling*". Insurers put large groups of similar people together, using common risk modelling points, and their premiums are used to fund a "common pool". In any given year, some will need to be paid out and some will not. As long as the common pool remains liquid – the system continues to work. Insurance based predictive analytics function by giving insurers more detail about individuals and associated risks. This allows for far more accurate risk pricing and removes the need to pool broad groups of people together.

Obviously this gives rise to a whole host of ethical questions about the availability and pricing of insurance as the technology leads us down the path of what has been referred to as "micro" pooling of insurance risk.

Car driving behaviours monitored by so called telematics "under the hood" black boxes are one obvious example which could lead to "risky" behaviours driving up insurance pricing and "safe" behaviours lowering it. Even more serious is the impact of advanced analytics on genetic data which might model susceptibility to genetic disease and therefore impact the pricing and availability of life insurance coverage.

Data Acquisition

Aside from predictive analytics, machine learning systems have a prodigious capacity to self-generate, collect and of course exchange data whilst they are being used (indeed, some devices, such as autonomous and semi-autonomous vehicles) are pro-actively designed on this basis. What the IAF neglects to include in its analysis is also the category of "*Generated*" data, although this might arguably fall within their category of "*Observed*" data.

Data generation, acquisition and exchange has already drawn the significant attention of regulators. The European Commission recently published its *Strategy on Co-Operative Intelligent Transport Systems or "CIT-S"*[37] which sets out its approach to developing a standardised intelligent transport infrastructure allowing vehicles to communicate with each other, with centralised traffic management systems and other highway users[38]. The potential for such data to be misused is clearly troubling – for example not only could a CAV identify a journey destination, it could also potentially also report back on driving habits (when not in autonomous mode) and theoretically identify any traffic offences.

In the context of our discussion such data could obviously also have an impact on the manner in which insurance is offered to the user of the vehicle when under human control.

To date, the policy adopted by the EU Commission has been to identify such data as personal data and therefore afford it the protection of the European data protection framework.

Understanding how AI systems Process Data

We tend to think of traditional computer data processing as the assimilation of large amounts of data which are then varied/changed/updated or adapted in some mechanistic way to support the application or program being utilised by the system.

In contrast, as I indicated in the introduction to this book and at the start of this particular chapter, the inherent value in most AI systems is in their ability to spot patterns, correlations and different dimensionalities in the data sets which they observe. Whilst this may not have a hugely practical consequence so far as the regulatory definitions of *"personal data"*[39] and

---

[37] See: http://ec.europa.eu/energy/sites/ener/files/documents/1_en_act_part1_v5.pdf

[38] Unfortunately plans to implement an EU wide Regulation embodying the principles of the CIT-S strategy have to date stalled, with the EU Council and Parliament objecting to the draft measure on the basis of its perceived lack of technological neutrality.

[39] Article 4(1) GDPR

"processing"[40] are concerned, it is conceptually important to understand this difference and it is a topic we will return to in the context of intellectual property and artificial intelligence later on in this book.

AI systems tend to observe, learn and model from the large data sets they are exposed to. The value in the utility of such systems is not therefore just in the sense that they can process the data elements in large data sets – it is also in their ability to spot and correlate patterns in such data and learn (or optimise output) through use of the *Learner* element of the system.

The closest analogy is of course a human being learning a new skill. A human will assimilate a skill from tangible materials (data) and training. Irrespective of whether those tangible materials (ie. the data elements) are returned to a third party, lost or subsequently destroyed, the skill and knowhow (or *learned* behaviours) still remain with the person.

The General Data Protection Regulation ("GDPR")

The GDPR ushers in a new era of responsibilities for those who control or process the personal data of EU citizens, and rights for those who are the subjects of such processing. Unfortunately, in pursuing the undoubtedly noble cause of protecting individual citizens the measure, as we shall see in a moment, also creates significant difficulties for the implementers users and owners of artificially intelligent systems – creating a "*Gordian knot*" of regulatory hurdles which often seem to be completely at odds with the practical implications (and business case benefits) of using such systems.

I do not propose in this section to provide a comprehensive guide to the measure which is far reaching beyond the confines of the immediate subject matter – but rather provide a view as to the issues which you will need to be aware of from a practical and conceptual basis when looking at AI systems that are designed to process personal data.

---

[40] Article 4(2) GDPR

It goes without saying that machine learning systems which do not process personal data are outside the scope of the legislation – however it pays to remember that personal data is not confined merely to data which refers *directly* or *overtly* to a living individual – the definition is wide enough to encompass data which could achieve such status through a process of *indirect* inference or derivation (see my previous comments under the heading of predictive analytics).

Key Concepts

Before we examine the impact of the GDPR on the users, implementers and owners of artificially intelligent computer systems, it is worth stepping through a few of the concepts which will define our debate. As before, this section will be necessarily led by the focus of this book – that is to say issues within the new EU regulation which are created or caused by artificial intelligence technologies.

"Fair" processing

At its heart, the GDPR mandates that all personal data should be processed *fairly*. Article 5(1)(a) provides that personal data must be *"processed fairly, lawfully and in a transparent manner in relation to the data subject."* As we have seen previously, it is the inherent complexity and "black box" nature of many AI system structures and architectures that causes considerable difficulties in the context of liability and causation. The position is no different in the context of data protection.

At its heart, the concept of fairness is driven by compliance with the Data Protection Principles[41] (which are largely unchanged from the prior regime under the Data Protection Directive) including the concept of transparency.

Transparency is a theme which runs through this narrative and in this context self-evidently refers to the manner in which the processing is publicised and clear to the data subject. This requirement generally refers to the purposes for which personal data are to be utilised, but as we shall see

---

[41] Article 5 (1) GDPR

in a little more detail later, it *also* refers to the way in which such data is *computationally* processed by the AI system.

Generally speaking, the requirement of transparency is achieved proce-durally under the GDPR by reference to the provision of *"fair processing"* or privacy information notices to the affected data subjects stating (*inter alia*) who the relevant parties are who will be controlling and processing their information, for what purposes it will be processed and who such data is going to be shared with. This however is but the starting point for such notices. There are significant practical and procedural difficulties applying this process to machine learning technologies, particularly given that the GDPR is much more prescriptive about how such notices should be designed and what they should (and should not) achieve, more of which we discuss below.

Data Processors or Data Controllers?

As with any technological system which makes use of Personal Data, the providers and users of machine learning systems need to evaluate the ex-tent to which they are Processors or Controllers of the personal data used by the system.

It is not the purpose of this book to provide a detailed explanation of each of these concepts but broadly speaking a Controller is a natural or legal person who determines the purposes and means of the data pro-cessing[42] and a Processor is a natural or legal person who processes per-sonal data on behalf of the Controller[43]. Often in the case of machine learning systems, the analysis as to whether the provider of the system is a Joint Controller with the user (rather than a Processor) can become quite complex issue to determine, particularly where personal data are ingested into a machine learning model as part of a training dataset to improve that system's output. Very often the answer is highly context specific and can hinge on issues such as the extent to which the model is

---

[42] Article 4(7)

[43] Article 4(8)

intended to be used for purposes additional to the original ones commissioned[44], or whether it is dedicated to a single use case.

Consent vs. Legitimate Interests

The lawfulness or otherwise of the relevant processing is also central to the regulatory framework. For the purposes of this debate, this will largely be driven by two of the concepts listed in Article 6 of the GDPR – either that "*the data subject has given consent to the processing of his or her personal data*"[45] or the "*processing is necessary for the purposes of the legitimate interests pursued by the controller... except where such interests are overridden by the interests or fundamental rights and freedoms of the data subject which require protection of personal data...*"

Under the data protection regime prior to the introduction of the GDPR, consent of the data subject had become somewhat of a discredited concept – many businesses had adopted the approach of burying general consent deep in a raft of obscure terms and conditions, or pre-populating check boxes, forcing data subjects to proactively "uncheck" in order *not* to give consent. Again, European legislators have effectively blocked these practices under the GDPR and strengthen the concept, stating that "*...Consent should be given by a clear affirmative act establishing a freely given specific, informed and unambiguous indication of the data subject's agreement as to the processing of personal data...this could include...conduct which clearly indicates in this context the data subject's acceptance of the proposed processing of his personal data. Silence, pre-ticked boxes or inactivity should not therefore constitute consent.*"[46]. The natural corollary of this of course is that the individual data subject is free to withdraw such consent at any time – indeed this is the position that is legislated for in Article 7(3) of the GDPR.

For the purposes of our current analysis, and indeed generally in relation

---

[44] Such as for example, where a supplier intends to use a model trained on data provided by one customer for its other customers.

[45] Article 6(1)a

[46] See Recital 32 of the GDPR

to all personal data processing based on this ground, it does of course mean that consent as a lawful basis for processing has been dramatically reduced in utility – on any objective basis, why go to the trouble of obtaining pro-active consent for processing in relation to a particular purpose – including significant levels of investment in systems and technology to carry out such activity if consent can be withdrawn at any time by any individual?

This practical problem with pro-active consent has meant that may businesses are now seeking to rely on *legitimate interests* instead as a lawful processing ground. It is this sea change in approach which is fuelling a healthy growth in GDPR audit assessment activity – because simply put, if a business seeks to rely on their *legitimate interests*, they must undertake a comprehensive and detailed assessment[47] which balances these interests with the rights and interests of the data subjects concerned. The point here is that the processing must be *necessary* for the data controller's legitimate interests, and not merely *convenient*. Article 13(1)d of the GDPR provides that where a data controller is relying on the legitimate interests ground, it must explain this in the relevant privacy information notice.

Profiling

Article 4(4) of the GDPR introduces the concept of *"profiling"* which will be of particular relevance to the use of AI systems evaluating and making decisions on data sets comprised of large amounts of personal data. This provides that profiling means *"any form of automated processing of personal data consisting of the use of personal data to evaluate certain aspects relating to a natural person, in particular to analyse or predict aspects concerning that natural person's performance at work, economic situation, health, personal preferences, interests, reliability, behaviour, location or movements"*.

The three key aspects of the profiling process are that it should be automated; carried out using personal data and utilised to evaluate personal aspects of a natural person. It is clear that the legislators intended this

---

[47] A so-called "DPIA" or Data Protection Impact Assessment

concept to be construed as widely as possible[48], so that whilst the decision making involved has to include some form of automated processing, it does not rule out human intervention per se. Equally speaking, profiling does not need to involve the higher predictive elements of a machine learning system – it can e.g. simply entail the classification of people in terms of their gender, race and interests.

Automated Decision Making

Article 22(1) introduces another key concept, that of automated decision making. This may or may not include profiling but is distinguished from the former as being performed solely by machine (ie with no human intervention).

The GDPR includes a right for data subjects *"not to be subject to a decision which is based solely on automated processing, including profiling, which produces legal effects concerning him or her or similarly significantly affects him or her."* The key point here is that if the automated decision making falls within the definition set out in Article 22, then legitimate interests cannot be used as a lawful processing ground and the redefined concept of consent, with all of its inherent weaknesses (at least from a business perspective), needs to be used instead. It is important to note however that not all machine learning decisions will be caught by this definition. There are several additional considerations to be taken into account before the Article 22 threshold is reached.

Solely Automated

The first requirement is that the automated decision making or profiling needs to be *"solely automated"*. What this means is that there is effectively no human involvement in the decision making or profiling process. In the world of big data this is a substantial concern for those businesses that work on a large scale. Artificially intelligent systems have the ability to substantially increase processing speed whilst retaining sophistication in

---

[48] See the Article 29 Working Party paper entitled "Guidelines on Automated individual decision making and Profiling for the purposes of Regulation 2016/679 (3 October 2017)

the assessments applied to such decisions. Without commenting on the socio-political and ethical aspects of such an approach, this is an undoubted technological advantage for those citizens who ultimately benefit and for whom the outcome would otherwise be delayed.

There has been much debate about what level of human "in the loop" involvement there needs to be to avoid this requirement and some clues are provided by the original Article 29 Working Party on this particular topic. In essence human involvement needs to be *meaningful*, as they state "*the controller cannot avoid the Article 22 provisions by fabricating human involvement*"[49].

Clearly, human involvement cannot be tokenised. It should be carried out by someone who has the authority to review and if necessary reverse that decision and who can also weigh all available data supporting it[50]. Care also needs to be given to natural human biases in this situation as well. This was considered by the UK's Information Commissioner in a 2019 AI related blog post[51], where the concepts of automation bias and lack of interpretability were considered as potential indicators which could cause a system to fall within the "*solely automated*" category.

Automation Bias

Automation bias refers to the natural human tendency to trust the outputs of models based on mathematics and data. The argument runs that in trusting such technologies, humans become complacent and stop using their own judgment to evaluate and assess outputs. In essence this is the paradigm expressed in comedic terms by the phrase "*Computer says*

---

[49] Guidelines on Automated individual decision-making and Profiling for the purposes of Regulation 2016/679, adopted 3rd October 2017

[50] Guidelines on Automated individual decision-making and Profiling for the purposes of Regulation 2016/679, adopted 3rd October 2017, page 21

[51] Automated Decision Making: the role of meaningful human reviews see: https://ico.org.uk/about-the-ico/news-and-events/ai-blog-automated-decision-making-the-role-of-meaningful-human-reviews/

no"[52]

Lack of Interpretability

Lack of interpretability in essence refers to the characteristics discussed elsewhere in this book of deep neural networks – that is to say their "black box" characteristics. The very fact that a human might find such a system difficult to interpret or challenge, because it cannot be easily understood, could lead it to become 'solely automated'.

Legal Effects

In addition to the 'solely automated' requirement, the automated decision making or profiling needs to have "legal effects" on the data subject concerned – these are relatively straightforward to categorise – they refer to decisions that impact the legal rights, status or rights under a contract of the affected data subject. The Article 29 Working Party provides examples of this such as the cancellation of contracts, denial of social benefit payments or even refusal of admission to a country[53].

Similarly Significant [Effects]

It is important to note however that the automated decision or profiling does not necessarily need to produce legal effects on a data subject to fall within its scope. Article 22 provides, somewhat inelegantly, that it can apply in circumstances where the decision *"similarly significantly affects him or her."* For ease of reference, I have referred to this impact as "Similarly Significant Effects".

What then are Similarly Significant Effects? These are outcomes which are broadly equivalent in their impact to legal effects. The concern of the legislators here is to protect data subjects from being prejudiced by automated decisions which will fundamentally affect them. Remember also that this analysis should not necessarily be confined solely to *"obtained"*

---

[52] First coined in the 2004 BBC TV comedy series *Little Britain*.

[53] Guidelines on Automated individual decision-making and Profiling for the purposes of Regulation 2016/679, adopted 3rd October 2017, page 21

data – it could also apply to data that has been *"derived"* or *"inferred"* – that is to say correlated indirectly without being proactively handed over by the data subject concerned.

Again the Article 29 Working Party provides useful examples[54] such as the automatic refusal of an online credit application or e-recruiting practices without human intervention. The decisions themselves need to have the potential to *"...significantly affect the circumstances, behaviour or choices of the individuals concerned; have a prolonged or permanent impact on the data subject; or at [their] most extreme, lead to the exclusion or discrimination of individuals..."*[55].

Very significantly (and perhaps even more problematically for our purposes) *Similiarly Significant Effects* are judged by reference to their subjective impact on the data subject and not by means of a generalised objective view of how they might have such impact (*not* in other words the achetypal *"man on the Clapham omnibus"*[56]). So for example, someone who is in a minority group, disabled, or is a child might be impacted more significantly than an able-bodied person or an adult[57]. Quite how this impact could be modelled on an operational basis for the purposes of AI systems remains largely unresolved.

Special Category Data

Finally, the concept of Special Category Data as that is defined in Article 9 of the GDPR needs to be considered, to the extent that this is relevant. Special Category Data are defined as the protected characteristics of an individual[58], including their race, ethnic origin, genetic data, biometric

---

[54] Ibid.

[55] Ibid.

[56] This is the hypothetical '*ordinary reasonable person*' standard adopted in many cases by English common law (see *Hall v. Brooklands Auto Racing Club* [1933] 1 KB 205)

[57] Guidelines on Automated individual decision-making and Profiling for the purposes of Regulation 2016/679, adopted 3rd October 2017, page 22

[58] See Article 9 (1)

data (when used for identification), health and sexual characteristics. The processing of these classes of personal data trigger enhanced protections under the GDPR due to their sensitivity, which generally prohibits any such activity unless certain limited exceptions apply, including as in the case of automated decision making, the explicit consent of the data subject.

Clearly, use of Special Category Data are a particular legal concern for applications such as Automated Facial Recognition, and I discuss some of the more specific concerns arising from use of that technology in Chapter four. For the purposes of this chapter however, it is important to remember that Special Category Data can also be subject to automated decision making and profiling under Article 22 of the GDPR.

Purpose limitation and data minimisation

The concepts covered by Articles 5(1)(b) and 5(1)(c) of the GDPR, which continue with the so called "*purpose limitation*" and "*data minimisation*" principles are also potential hurdles to the implementation of certain classes of machine learning systems. They explicitly provide that personal data should be "*collected for specified and legitimate purpose and not further processed in a manner which is incompatible with those purposes*" and it should also be "*adequate, relevant and limited to what is necessary in relation to the purposes for which they are processed*".

As we discussed earlier, it is self-evident that these requirements *could* potentially impede the use of unsupervised machine learning (the so called Rumsfeldian "*unknown knowns*"[59]) in a big data context. Such systems generate potentially useful analysis or correlation of data sets in circumstance that could not reasonably have been predicted or anticipated at the outset (such as the example quoted at the beginning of this chapter in relation to facial characteristics leading to a correlation in sexuality).

---

[59] Also referred to (and potentially inspired by) a poem by D.H. Lawrence – *New Heaven and Earth*

Privacy by Design

The final concept that is worth discussing in this section is that of *"privacy by design"*. This approach, which is mandated by the GDPR[60], was not a requirement of the prior Data Protection Directive. Encouragingly, it is this principle which may assist the users and owners of machine learning systems that have a personal data impact.

What privacy by design (technically *"privacy by design and privacy by default"*) requires is a structured design approach when creating a new information processing system. This means enshrining the concept of data privacy at its heart, rather than bolting it on as an afterthought which is so often the case in system architecture design. Often this will entail a root and branch analysis of the operational and ethical reasons why the personal data are needed and a full understanding of the impact of such data collection on the potential data subjects. The Privacy Commissioner of Ontario in Canada has published what is widely regarded as the leading conceptual approach in achieving privacy by design, by setting out seven foundational principles which should be at the heart of any such approach[61].

A first step on the path towards achieving privacy by design is by use of what are known as Privacy Impact Assessments (or DPIAs) (which are not to be confused with Privacy information notices). Article 35 of the GDPR provides that *"Where a type of processing in particular using new technologies, and taking into account the nature, scope, context and purposes of the processing, is likely to result in a high risk to the rights and freedoms of natural persons, the Controller shall, prior to the processing, carry out an assessment of the impact of the envisaged processing operations on the protection*

---

[60] Article 25 GDPR

[61] See *Privacy by Design, A Primer by the Ontario Privacy Commissioner.* Broadly speaking the seven principles accord with the general approach outlined above – by defining e.g. a proactive, not a reactive approach, making privacy a default setting, embedding privacy into the solution design, applying a positive sum (not a zero sum) approach, providing for full lifecycle protection, keeping use of data visible and transparent and ensuring respect for user privacy.

of personal data."[62]

Understanding information flows – what is collected and when, how it stored and for what purposes and how such data is computationally processed through the relevant system are a key part of such analysis. As we have previously discussed, any difficulties in explaining the computational processes of a *"black box"* AI system will therefore need to be balanced very carefully with cogent, ethical and logical reasons for such collection and processing, which can significantly justify the benefits of using such a system for the relevant data processing application.

Privacy information notices

All of this brings us back to the GDPR requirement that we discussed at the beginning of this chapter of ensuring *transparency* in processing by use of privacy information or *"fair processing"* notices.

As you will recall, these are required whether a business is seeking to rely on the *legitimate interests* or *consent* ground for lawful processing. Whilst admirable as a concept, such notices have the potential to create substantial difficulties in the context of artificial intelligence and machine learning, especially bearing in mind the complexity and *"black box"* nature of such systems.

Articles 12, 13 and 14 of the GDPR provide a particularly clear example of the potentially irreconcilable tautologies involved, by stipulating on the one hand that such notices should be "*...concise, transparent, intelligible and easily accessible...using clear and plain language...*"[63] whilst on the other hand stating that where automated decision making and/or profiling is involved that "*...meaningful information about the logic involved...*"[64] is also supplied. This is evidently not an easy tightrope to negotiate – particularly in a machine learning context. The logical first approach might be to provide a detailed explanation for the data subject

---

[62] Article 35(1) GDPR

[63] Article 12(1) GDPR

[64] Articles 13(2)(f) and 14(2)(g) GDPR

setting out the context and grounds for the processing and explaining in detail the computational details of the AI system being used, however this is likely to have the opposite effect of confusing the data subject or over-loading them with information. Indeed, the Article 29 Working Party has specifically stated that "*information fatigue*" should be avoided[65].

With perhaps a nod to this tautology, the framers of the legislation have indicated that there are various mechanisms which can be used to high-light in a user-friendly way, the information which is required to be con-veyed to the users of such systems.

The first accessible method which could be used is to implement clear iconography (on the basis that 'a picture is worth a thousand words') into the relevant privacy information notice. The use of icons is not a new approach, however the key has been to develop a consistent set of symbols which have an apparent individual meaning and read consistently with each other – often easier said than done. The GDPR provides a mecha-nism for the introduction of standardised icons under Article 12(8), but as yet there are no agreed forms.

The second method is very much context driven and depends upon the nature of the system involved and the manner in which personal data are to be collected. It is however of relevance to complex information pro-cessing systems and relies on making relevant information available to the data subject when it is needed, rather than in one large undigestible no-tice up front. "*Just in time*" notices (as they are referred to) rely on state-ments on information processing being given at the time a relevant ques-tion is being asked of an individual (through the use e.g. of pop-up or pop-over dialogue boxes). These can be coupled with an approach with allows for "*layering*" – basic information being made available with a "*click through*" link for those users who desire to have access to more de-tailed information about the manner in which their data will be pro-cessed.

It does not take a lot of imagination to see that innovative adoption of

---

[65] See Paragraph 7 of the Article 29 Working Party paper on Transparency 17/EN WP260

these techniques (which whilst potentially difficult to conceptualise at the outset), may provide implementers of machine learning systems with a route through the potentially conflicting requirements of Articles 12, 13 & 14 of the GDPR.

The Data Protection Act 2018

The UK's separation from the European Union, or Brexit as it has commonly become known, adds unfortunately another degree of complexity to what is an undoubtedly a difficult legislative context to navigate for the users of machine learning systems.

The new Data Protection Act (the "DPA 2018"), which was enacted into law synchronously with the General Data Protection Regulation on May 25th 2018, aims to enshrine the essential principles of the GDPR into UK law post-Brexit. Sadly, the post-Brexit legislative map for data in the UK is somewhat confused now, as the position is governed not only by the DPA 2018, but also by what is termed the 'UK GDPR'. Essentially a parallel version of the EU GDPR which has been adjusted to conform to UK domestic law[66]. It is beyond the scope of this work to delve into the complexities of the interaction between these measures, however it is worth highlighting a couple of measures in the DPA 2018.

Unfortunately, in the legislators' assiduous attempts to "*gold plate*" the UK's data protection compliance (no doubt fostered by a desire to attain equivalence with the remaining member states of the EU in terms of data transfers), the measure includes some criminal sanctions for companies and somewhat more worryingly, personal criminal sanctions for company directors. Whilst the Act does not provide for custodial sentences on breach (the sanctions are in essence limited to fines), these new offences will no doubt add a degree of real anxiety, given the irreconcilable tautologies in the GDPR we have discussed above, to those who seek to use and implement machine learning solutions post-Brexit.

It is worthwhile considering two in particular that have been introduced

---

[66] The relevant amendments are made by s3 of the European Union (Withdrawal) Act 2018

in relation to personal data and understanding their potential implications for artificial intelligence.

Unlawful obtaining of personal data

The Act provides in section 170 that *"it is an offence for a person knowingly or recklessly (a) to obtain or disclose personal data without the consent of the controller, (b) to procure the disclosure of personal data to another person without the consent of the controller, or (c) after obtaining personal data, to retain it without the consent of the person who was the controller in relation to the personal data when it was obtained."*[67]. Sub-sections (1) and (2) provide for various defences, including in relation to the prevention or detection of crime; for the purposes of law or court order; and justified disclosure in the public interest. It is also a defence if you can show that the controller would have consented had they known or if you had a reasonable (if incorrect) belief that you were authorised to disclose. This offence is similar to the one in the previous 1998 Data Protection Act – however it is extended to include the retention of personal data. As we discuss in the context of intellectual property in Chapter five (see under the paragraph headed *"The learned behaviours paradigm"*), there is a tendency of machine learning systems to retain what I have described as *"information residuals"* – principally the associative and correlative aspects describing statistical patterns and correlations in data used by the system (rather than the content of that data itself) – being retained by the machine learning system in an analogous fashion to a taught human being. The simple anthropomorphic analogy is that once something is learned, it cannot be unlearned. Clearly personal data processed by machine learning systems can be returned once it has been used – the question is whether what remains – the *information residuals* – constitutes retention for the purposes of this offence.

Re-identification of de-identified personal data

Section 171 creates an offence of re-identification of de-identified personal data: *"(1) It is an offence for a person knowingly or recklessly to re-identify information that is de-identified personal data without the consent*

---

[67] Section 170(1) of the Data Protection Act 2018

of the controller responsible for de-identifying the personal data. ... (a) personal data is "de-identified" if it has been processed in such a manner that it can no longer be attributed, without more, to a specific data subject; (b) a person "re-identifies" information if the person takes steps which result in the information no longer being de-identified within the meaning of paragraph (a)"[68]. This offence is aimed at protecting data which has been *pseudonymised* (where re-identification is possible) (as opposed to fully anonymised where it should be impossible to re-identify data subjects). Users of machine learning systems should be mindful of the powerful ability of such systems to apply predictive analytics to the data that they process (see earlier in this chapter under the heading *"Predictive Analytics"*). In the context of our immediate debate the risk must be to prevent or at least put in place measures to avoid a machine learning system from *deriving* or *inferring* sufficient characteristics in the data it processes to inadvertently re-identify data subjects.

Open Data

Moving away from the UK's post-Brexit data legislation, it is worth now covering developments in Open Data.

It is an oft quoted fact that more data has been created by humans in the past two years than the entire previous history of the human race.[69] And yet we live and work in a fragmented data world with little or no consistency in the way data are shared as between individuals, enterprise and nation states.

"Open Data" initiatives are the response to this fragmentation. They are driven by the recognition that the removal of "data siloes" will benefit society generally by improving access to information (and all the associated benefits that will bring, such as increased transparency and accountability) and will accelerate progress and innovation in specific technologies such as artificial intelligence and machine learning, which themselves

---

[68] Section 171(1) & (2) of the Data Protection Act 2018

[69] See for example *Big Data: 20 Mind-Boggling Facts Everyone Must Read*, Bernard Marr https://www.forbes.com/sites/bernardmarr/2015/09/30/big-data-20-mind-boggling-facts-everyone-must-read/?sh=3080bec717b1

depend upon data.

Put simply, Open Data encompasses the initiatives that are taking place globally to share and improve access to data. In this part of the chapter we'll take a look at some of the steps that are being taken to facilitate open access to data.

The EU's Strategy for Data

The European Union has long taken the concept of Open Data seriously. As far back as 2003, it enacted a measure referred to as the Public Sector Information or PSI Directive[70], which was ultimately replaced by the Open Data Directive[71]. The Open Data Directive focusses on the economic aspects of the re-use of public information as an EU-wide resource, rather than on access to information by European Citizens. It has now taken the concept of Open Data further, in part driven by the imperative of putting in place a complementary coherent strategy for artificial intelligence and machine learning technologies. Indeed the European Data Strategy[72] was launched at the same time as the White Paper on Artificial Intelligence which is discussed extensively elsewhere in this book.

What the strategy aims to achieve is the facilitation of a "single market" for data, which should be able to flow freely within the EU and across different market sectors. One of the ways it proposes to achieve this is by the creation of common European "data spaces" in strategic sectors, such as industrial manufacturing, mobility, health, financial, agriculture, public adminstration and skills[73]. As the Commission itself states "…*This should lead to the availability of large pools of data in these sectors and domains, combined with the technical tools and infrastructures necessary to use and exchange data…*"[74].

---

[70] Directive 2003/98

[71] Directive 2019/1024

[72] A European Strategy for data, Brussels 19.2.2020, COM(2020) 66 final – see https://ec.europa.eu/info/sites/info/files/communication-european-strategy-data-19feb2020_en.pdf

[73] Ibid., page 22-23

[74] Ibid., page 21

EU Data Governance Act

The first draft Regulation announced as part of the EU strategy, the so-called Data Governance Act[75] was published on 25th November 2020. The Data Governance Act aims to improve data governance mechanisms and implement data sharing mechanisms across the EU.

The UK National Data Strategy

In a similar fashion, the UK government kicked off its National Data Strategy consultation on 9th September 2020, which was open for consultation until 9th December 2020. The consultation will inform the National Data Strategy Framework[76], currently under review. The aim of the strategy is to provide a trusted ecosystem within the UK for data sharing and access.

Data Trusts

The term "Data Trust" was first coined in a 2017 report[77] prepared by Dame Wendy Hall (professor of Computer Science at the University of Southampton) and Jérôme Pesenti (chief executive of BenevolentTech) as part of a review into the UK's Artificial Intelligence industry.

Data Trusts were conceived as an approach to replicate the traditional characteristics and benefits of trusts to the stewardship and custody of data. The concept entails one party authorising another the "*data trustee*" to make decisions about data on their behalf, often for the benefit of a wider group of "*data beneficiaries*" or stakeholders. The idea follows that like a traditional trust, the data trustee would assume a fiduciary duty

---

[75] See https://ec.europa.eu/digital-single-market/en/news/data-governance-act

[76] See https://www.gov.uk/government/publications/uk-national-data-strategy/national-data-strategy

[77] *Growing the Artificial Intelligence Industry in the UK* – Otherwise known as the Hall-Pesenti Review

towards the ultimate data beneficiaries[78].

As at the date of writing, there is no legislation in the UK or elsewhere in the world to formalise the concept of data trusts, so the idea remains theoretical. The UK's Open Data Institute however has provided examples of entities that operate in an analogous manner, such as the UK Biobank which was set up to steward genetic data and is constituted as a charitable company[79]. There are also moves in private enterprise to set up digitally framed data trusts. Sightline Innovation for example, a Canadian based business, has set up what it calls a trusted data collaboration platform which is designed to operate in much the same manner as a data trust, enabling interoperability whilst maintaining data compliance and governance[80].

Data Intermediaries

Aside from the data trust model, there are many other forms of what I have termed "data intermediary" that are positioning themselves as trusted data interchanges.

One of the key challenges in enabling a form of digitalised data exchange is the reality that aside from the fact that much data is held in fragmented silos, the format of the data itself is incompatible and does not lend itself to sharing. As such the market has turned to solutions that are attempting to provide a standardised data interchange format as a prelude to fully digitalised sharing.

One such business, EngineB[81] is focussed on just this task and is developing what it terms common data models for the flow of data between audit, legal and tax professionals and their clients. The theory is that by standardising the data used by law firms and accountancy practices, it

---

[78] See What is a Data Trust: www. https://theodi.org/article/what-is-a-data-trust

[79] Ibid.

[80] See www.sightlineinnovation.com

[81] See www.engineb.com

will be much easier for clients to change their professional services advisors (this could conceivably be done by the flick of a proverbial switch). The other advantage is that audit businesses could simply monitor in real time the bank transactions of an audited business to evaluate against tax and other reporting governance rules, as well as apply all of the powerful benefits of data analytics discussed earlier in this chapter.

Data Commons

Finally, it is worth discussing the concept of Data Commons. This is a term which has been coined to refer to an open data licensing framework which is based upon similar principles to Open Source Software licensing. A particular example of this approach is the one adopted by the Linux Foundation[82], which has developed a Community Data License Agreement[83]. The Linux Foundation CDLA is essentially split into two forms. The CLDA-Sharing[84] license embodies the principles of "copyleft"[85] in a data licence, in essence providing that downstream recipients can use and modify that data (and are also required to share their changes to that data) and the CDLA-Permissive[86] license, which allows modification of data without any obligation to share such changes or modifications.

---

[82] https://www.linuxfoundation.org/

[83] https://cdla.dev/

[84] https://cdla.dev/sharing-1-0/

[85] Copyleft is the practice of granting the right to freely distribute and modify intellectual property with the requirement that the same rights be preserved in derivative works created from that property.

[86] https://cdla.dev/permissive-1-0/

CHAPTER FOUR
AUTOMATED FACIAL
RECOGNITION

As I emphasised in the foreword to this edition, automated facial recognition technologies (or "*AFR*") have recently garnered significant public attention and comment. Technological advances in artificial intelligence and machine learning have dramatically improved the utility of AFR which is increasingly being deployed in both commercial and state sponsored contexts.

Whilst it is true to say that the legal position in relation to automated facial recognition is evolving, it is not correct to assume that there is no regulation. AFR technology sits in a complex regulatory area which is a fusion of artificial intelligence, data processing, biometric data handling and surveillance, justifying a chapter in its own right.

By its nature, much of the existing law applicable to AFR is "use case" dependent and will apply differently, for example, if you are using the technology as part of an active video surveillance application, querying a pre-existing facial database, or a combination of both.

Different laws and codes of conduct will apply depending upon the extent to which a particular facial recognition application is used on public or private property and, of course, state actors such as the police, counter-terrorism and intelligence services will be bound by a separate regime. In such cases the Regulation of Investigatory Powers Act 2000, the Intelligence Services Act 1994 and Part III of the Police Act 1997 together put in place a regulatory framework for state actors, principally around the gathering and retention of covert investigative information, to determine proportionality and necessity, as well as intrusive interference in relation to real property and voice and data networks – by definition this includes the operation of "covert" AFR systems.

This book is not intended to focus on the state-sponsored use of AFR technologies, but you need to be mindful that separate rules exist to cover such use and by definition often permit activities which are beyond mere commercial use.

The Investigatory Powers Commissioners Office[87] has regulatory oversight over law enforcement users and use of such data, as well as the Law Enforcement Facial Images and New Biometrics Oversight and Advisory Board[88].

Misuse of AFR taps into wider public unease over the covert use and capturing of such biometric data and has the potential to cause serious reputational damage to a business (or state authority) if it fails to sensitively take into account the wider societal implications of use – let alone the narrower regulatory implications.

Recent studies have also indicated that the technology may not be as accurate as initially thought, an issue which was considered, in the case of *R (Bridges) v. Chief Constable of South Wales Police*[89], discussed further below. This makes any use case evaluation of AFR even more important.

Data Protection

Any analysis of the compliance of an AFR system will inevitably need to start with an assessment of its adherence to the data protection regime under the General Data Protection Regulation (the "GDPR") and Data Protection Act 2018 ("DPA 2018"), and relevant guidance issued by the Information Commissioner's Office ("ICO").

Facial images themselves are classed as personal data (i.e. data that can

---

[87] See www.ipco.org.uk

[88] This has been suspended as at the date of writing. The government website (https://www.gov.uk/government/groups/law-enforcement-facial-images-and-new-biometrics-oversight-and-advisory-board) states rather unhelpfully "*The Law Enforcement Facial Images and New Biometrics Oversight and Advisory Board oversaw the police use of automated facial recognition (AFR), live facial recognition (LFR) custody images and new biometrics. The last meeting of the Board took place in September 2019 and alternative governance arrangements are now in place.*"

[89] [2020] EWCA Civ 1058

readily identify individuals) but processing by an AFR system brings with it extra stringent regulation. As we discussed in Chapter three, this is because biometric facial data used to *uniquely identify* an individual[90] is classified as *special category data*, or sensitive data. The general principle here is that such data cannot be processed under the legitimate interests lawful processing ground: explicit consent needs to be relied upon instead.

In addition to these considerations, it is likely that the AFR application will be relying on some form of automated processing, so considerations raised by Article 22 of the GDPR will also need to be factored in.

All of the above raises substantial conceptual issues about the extent to which it is actually feasible to implement the technology within the EU (and now, post-Brexit, the UK) as in many use cases of AFR, individuals are instantly recognised by such systems long before they have the opportunity to pro-actively consent to their facial data being processed. In a sense this is another manifestation of the structural difficulties that the GDPR has with artificial intelligence and machine learning that I have highlighted elsewhere in this book.

To take a particular example, in the United States, Amazon has been rolling out a chain of stores branded *"Amazon Go"*. These are physical stores which typically carry groceries. Shoppers simply enter and take goods from the shelves – there is no checkout process. Instead, that is handled by Amazon's facial recognition algorithms. Shoppers registered on Amazon's Go app are recognised by Amazon's systems as they enter the Go store, and their account is automatically debited when they leave with their selected items[91].

Applying that example to the EU (and by extension the UK), it would seem apparent that proactive consent could be obtained through the Amazon Go app, but what of shoppers who enter the store and are not

---

[90] Article 9(1) GDPR

[91] See *How 'Amazon Go' works: The technology behind the online retailer's groundbreaking new grocery store* https://www.geekwire.com/2016/amazon-go-works-technology-behind-online-retailers-groundbreaking-new-grocery-store/

registered with Amazon at all? The mere fact that the AFR system scans their face in an attempt to identify whether or not they are a registered customer puts the retailer into breach of its obligations under the GDPR as such people will not have been given the opportunity to consent (or decline) to have their facial images scanned. This is of course before consideration is given to facial data which may be acquired from demographic groups that require even more special consideration under the GDPR, such as children, who may lack the capacity to provide effective consent.

Attempts to introduce the technology thus far in the UK have been limited to security-based applications, for what seem to be precisely these reasons.

Facewatch[92], a UK business targeted on retail loss prevention, relies on the *substantial public interest* exception to the consent provisions of the UK DPA on the basis that such use cases are justified in the public interest to prevent the commission of crime (in this case, shoplifting). This approach has yet to be substantively tested in the Courts.

Other substantive issues to be considered include ensuring that the application is designed with a view to maintaining privacy (referred to as "*privacy by design*"). It is also best practice in such circumstances to ensure that a comprehensive data protection impact assessment is carried out as such processing is likely to have a high degree of impact on affected individuals[93]. Indeed the UK's ICO has made it clear that this must be carried out by law enforcement when live facial recognition technology is used in public places[94].

---

[92] www.facewatch.co.uk

[93] See Article 35(3) of the GDPR which requires a DPIA when there are "*systematic and extensive evaluation of personal aspects based on automated processing, including profiling, on which decisions are made that produce legal or similarly significant effects; large-scale processing of special categories of personal data; or systematic monitoring of publicly-accessible areas on a large scale*"

[94] See Information Commissioner's Opinion: The use of live facial recognition technology by law enforcement in public places, 31 October 2019 Reference: 2019/01

Understanding how AFR data will be held and processed is thus vital to determining the legality of any particular use case.

Human Rights

Turning to Human Rights, Article 8 of the European Convention of Human Rights ("ECHR") provides for a right to respect for one's private and family life, home and correspondence and is directly actionable under English law through the mechanism of the Human Rights Act 1998. The right is clearly designed to circumscribe and limit intrusive activity which could damage privacy.

Although clearly applicable to "state sponsored" uses, it is wise to consider these principles in a private sector context and to consider how an AFR application might interfere with those rights in such situations.

Current police trials of AFR have been subject to challenge by human rights organisations on this basis (as we will discuss shortly in the context of the *South Wales Police* case).

Protection of Freedoms Act

Chapter 2 of Part 1 of the Protection of Freedoms Act 2012 ("PFA 2012")[95] provides for oversight by the Biometrics Commissioner of certain biometric data gathered under the Police and Criminal Evidence Act 1998 – principally fingerprints, DNA samples and custody pictures but increasingly also facial databases (such as the National Police Database) maintained by law enforcement authorities. Chapter 1 of Part 2 (s33) of the PFA 2012 governs the use and regulation of CCTV and other surveillance camera technology by "*relevant authorities*" (principally state actors), and provides for the Surveillance Camera Commissioner, of which more below.

---

https://ico.org.uk/media/about-the-ico/documents/2616184/live-frt-law-enforce-ment-opinion-20191031.pdf

[95] https://www.legislation.gov.uk/ukpga/2012/9/contents/enacted

Surveillance Camera Code of Practice

The Surveillance Camera Code of Practice 2013[96] ("SCC Code") applies to the use of "overt" video surveillance systems in public places by relevant public authorities, where compliance is mandatory. Chapter 4 (and Principle 12 specifically) refer to the use and/or processing of images obtained by CCTV. The code is administered by the Surveillance Camera Commissioner ("SCC").

Where AFR is used as part of a public authority administered public scheme, the SCC will have jurisdiction and can enforce compliance with the SCC Code. The SCC's mission is to ensure voluntary compliance with the SCC Code by unregulated (private) entities, so although not directly applicable in such circumstances, it is still a factor that needs to be considered.

Equality Act

If the use of AFR could produce biased outcomes (in particular through use of facial training data that does not adequately represent the ethnic diversity of modern society) then it pays also to be mindful of the impact and consequences of the Equality Act 2010[97] ("EA 2010") and in particular the need to avoid both direct and indirect discrimination. Again, these are concepts which are discussed more substantively in Chapter six on Bias and Discrimination. This particular aspect of AFR system use was discussed at length in the *South Wales Police* case.

Private Security Industry Act

Finally, the use of AFR which involves a security application extending to public spaces and which includes CCTV monitoring and/or door supervision, may constitute a licensable activity under the Private

---

[96] https://assets.publishing.service.gov.uk/government/uploads/system/uploads/attach-ment_data/file/282774/SurveillanceCameraCodePractice.pdf

[97] https://www.legislation.gov.uk/ukpga/2010/15/contents

Security Industry Act 2001[98].

This legislation was originally enacted to provide a licensing regime for the private security industry which had suffered from a poor reputation previously. Licences are administered by the Security Industry Authority[99] ("SIA"). Failure to obtain a licence, when one is needed, is a criminal offence which may be punishable by fines and/or imprisonment.

Facial recognition decisions

So that was a high level view of the relevant legislative framework applying to commercial use cases.

What then of the applicable case law? As you would imagine this is currently sparse. As at the date of writing, there are two significant European decisions, and one significant US based settlement – each leading to different conclusions, although each justifiably distinguishable on its facts.

R (Bridges) v. Chief Constable of South Wales Police

The South Wales Police case is a UK Court of Appeals case which was concluded in August 2020. The case itself is interesting as an insight into the thinking of the UK Court of Appeals although the principles arising from it in relation to AFR are necessarily limited to use by public sector organisations and therefore will be of limited application to private sector use. The case was determined under the prior UK data protection regime (as governed by the Data Protection Act 1998), but the court was also asked to look at what the outcome might have been under the new DPA 2018.

In this case, the South Wales Police ("SWP") were using an AFR pilot in Swansea city centre to match a "watchlist" of felons, suspects and other persons of interest to their facial database. Crucially for the purpose of their analysis, the police immediately deleted facial data in respect of

---

[98] https://www.legislation.gov.uk/ukpga/2001/12/contents

[99] https://www.gov.uk/government/organisations/security-industry-authority

unknown people and only retained data relating to facial matches. The plaintiff, Ed Bridges, had brought an appeal against an earlier Divisional Court judgment on a number of grounds challenging the lawfulness of SWP's use of the technology as a person in the vicinity of the SWP's AFR vans when in use.

The Court of Appeal agreed with the Divisional Court judgment which held that there had been interference with the appellant's Human Rights – specifically Article 8 of the ECHR, however crucially they disagreed with the lower court's assessment that the underlying law was sufficient to justify its use within Article 8(2). As the Data Protection Impact Assessment prepared by the SWP under s64 of the DPA 2018 had incorrectly concluded that there was no infringement of Article 8, the court found in consequence that it had failed to properly address the risks arising from the use of the AFR system.

At the core of the judgment were concerns that this insufficiency in law inadequately dealt with what the Court termed the "*who*" question (ie who should be identified as a "person of interest" on the SWP watchlist) and the "*where*" question (ie where deployment of AFR would be justified). Currently too much discretion was accorded to individual police officers in determining these issues (indeed the court referred to the discretion here as "*impermissibly wide*"). In terms of the existing legal framework the Court's view was that whilst the DPA 2018 formed an important part of the framework it was not sufficient by itself, and whilst the SCC Code briefly mentioned AFR, it did not deal specifically with these fundamental "*who*" and "*where*" issues.

Finally, and perhaps most controversially for the use of AFR in public sector contexts, the court held that in its use of the technology the SWP had not met its Public Sector Equality Duty (or "*PSED*"), in accordance with s149(1) of the EA 2010.

The PSED is designed amongst other things to ensure that public sector authorities eliminate discrimination, harrassment, victimisation and any other conduct prohibited by the EA 2010. In sharp contradiction to the earlier Divisional Court judgment, the Court of Appeal held that SWP had failed the standard of the PSED by not investigating (or even considering) the potential for the AFR system to produce biased outcomes in relation to BAME community members.

There were many issues which were frustratingly not dealt with in a conclusive manner by the South Wales Police judgment. In particular the key dichotomy of consent vs. legitimate interests as lawful processing grounds discussed earlier was sidestepped due to the law enforcement nature of the use case[100]. It is also apparent that the court's assessment of the insufficiency of the legal framework supporting public sector use of AFR will very likely lead to further legislative and policy interventions.

Skellefteå School Board

The Skellefteå School Board case[101] was a decision of the Swedish Data Protection Authority, Datainspektionen, a year ealier than *South Wales Police*, in August 2019.

In this case it was subsequently discovered that Anderstorps upper secondary school in the Swedish municipality of Skellefteå had been using facial recognition technology in a trial to log school students for attendance purposes. The pilot use of the technology had also been implemented in an attempt to speed up and automate the daily registration process. Biometric data from students was captured in the form of photographs and associated with their full names. Consent had been obtained from the parents and/or legal guardians of the children concerned.

Ultimately the School was fined SEK 200,000 (around £17,000). The

---

[100] The court of appeal judgment specifically pointed to three paragraphs in Schedule 2 of the DPA 1998 justifying use – Paragraph 3 – Processing necessary for compliance with a legal obligation other than one arising from contract; Paragraph 5(d) – processing necessary for the exercise of a function of a public nature, exercised in the public interest; and Paragraph 6 – processing necessary for legitimate interests of the data controller, and not unwarranted by reason of interference with the data subject's rights, freedoms or legitimate interests. See paragraph 126 of the official judgment transcript per Lord Justice Haddon-Cave and Mr. Justice Swift

[101] See https://www.imy.se/globalassets/dokument/beslut/facial-recognition-used-to-monitor-the-attendance-of-students.pdf

Swedish DPA found that an inadequate form of risk assessment had been carried out with no data protection impact assessment had been carried out and that contrary to Article 35 there was no formal data protection impact assessment. In addition it found that the processing of the children's biometric data was intrusive, and disproportionate, and could have been achieved in a less intrusive manner, contrary to Article 5 of the GDPR.

On the issue of consent, Datainspektionen found that notwithstanding that such had been obtained from parents and guardians, this could not be relied upon as there was an inequality of relationship between the Children and the School Board (such that any consent would have been brought into doubt).

Everalbum

In the United States the FTC[102] recently reached a settlement with a Calfornia-based developer of a photo app that it alleged had deceived consumers about the use of facial recognition technology[103], namely by not obtaining their consent to the acquistion of their biometric AFR data and also retaining it in circumstances where consumers had requested account deletion, in direct contravention of assurances made that such data would be deleted.

The settlement mandated that Everalbum, Inc. should obtain consumers express consent before using AFR on their photos and videos. What was also very notable was that the FTC mandated the a very wide deletion sanction: not just removal of the AFR data itself, but also the deletion of models and algorithms trained on the illegally applied AFR technology.

All of this does mean that applying AFR in both the public and private sectors remains a complex, evolving and delicate exercise wherever it is

---

[102] Federal Trade Commission

[103] See *California Company Settles FTC Allegations It Deceived Consumers about use of Facial Recognition in Photo Storage App* 11th January 2021, https://www.ftc.gov/news-events/press-releases/2021/01/california-company-settles-ftc-allegations-it-deceived-consumers

used. The utility of the technology needs to be balanced with thorny and substantial issues involving individual liberty and personal privacy.

CHAPTER FIVE
INTELLECTUAL PROPERTY
RIGHTS IN AI SYSTEMS

Traditionally intellectual property (or "*IP*") concepts form part of our established methods of protection for new technologies. In this chapter, we'll take a look at how IP can and cannot be used to protect investment and innovation in the development of artificial intelligence. We'll also consider whether intellectual property conventions, as in the context of causation earlier, may be breaking down, or at least fraying at the edges.

Before we examine some of the IP frameworks which might be applicable to machine learning, it is worthwhile taking some time to assess where the perceived *inherent value* in such technology lies, because in simple terms, if we can defend the valuable elements, we are more effectively protecting our entire AI asset. These considerations are clearly not only important from the perspective of the users and licensors of such technology, but also those who wish to obtain such systems through corporate activity (such as mergers and acquisitions).

As we learned in Chapter one, AI systems are not radically different from traditional computer systems in that they are essentially composed of two elements – the software which embodies the relevant AI model, and the computational hardware upon which it sits. Of course computational systems that host complex deep learning AI models are very sophisticated and can access huge amounts of processing power as well as harnessing petabytes of data – but they are still computers in the conventional sense.

At a superficial level one might say therefore that nothing has changed from an IP perspective, and that these are trite and settled issues: the computational hardware per se or in combination with software might in theory be eligible for patent protection under the Patents Act 1977, but that would require the elements of that Act to be made out – principally the element of industrial application[104] which requires a physical device or apparatus together with newness and an *inventive step* taking the physical device beyond the published *state of the art*[105].

Patents

Inventors of AI systems typically face real difficulties when looking to the Patents regime for legal protection. The first is that in many jurisdictions, including the UK and EU *disembodied software* is explicitly excluded from the scope of patent protection.

Then you have the problem of abstraction – in essence related to the problem of disembodied software – which is that if something is too abstract or can only be carried out in the human mind or as explained by the US patent office by a human being "*with pen and paper*", then it is not capable of protection. The European Patent office refers this as a scheme or rules and methods for performing mental acts. Finally, mathematical methods, such as algorithms per se are also excluded from scope.

You can see therefore that there are some quite considerable conceptual difficulties in getting a patent in relation to something which is potentially software related and highly abstract.

Despite these difficulties, machine learning patents are growing internationally at quite a phenomenal rate. Lots of efforts are expended as the 20-year monopoly period granted over patented technology is an extremely valuable right to have.

So how are potential patent owners getting around these difficulties? Well the first point to make in this regard is that entities with deep pockets will sometimes take a "*brute force*" approach – that is to say they will deluge the relevant patent office with so many applications that ultimately some will be granted. This is perhaps oversimplifying the position however: a granted patent is not necessarily a valid patent – only a court

---

[104] See s1(1)(c) Patents Act 1977

[105] See s1(1)(b) Patents Act 1977

can uphold validity after a patent challenge.

The European Patent Office (EPO) and US Patent and Trademark office (USPTO) each have their own attitude, policy and approach in relation to patent examination and registration. Any successful application will obviously need to conform to this. Historically the view has always been that it is anecdotally easier to have your software related invention patented in the United States – but current trends do not necessarily reflect this, with the EPO certainly becoming more receptive to applied AI use cases.

The most important barrier to break through is of course making sure that your invention is not classified as *"software"*. This is where the concept of the *"Computer Implemented Invention"* or CII has arisen. In essence this is a term which has been developed on a semantic sense to avoid the use of "*software*" in patents.

Merely referring to CII in an application is not sufficient however – the propose invention needs to critically have a "*technical effect*". What this means in very simple and general terms is that the system needs to manifest in a way that goes beyond the abstract – or at least be expressed in the application as having a technical effect which goes beyond the purely abstract. A simple example might be something that uses machine learning to actuate a robot limb or generate synthetic speech. Obviously this is not a binary analysis – so there are likely to be areas which are highly abstract but which do get granted patent protection, merely through the manner in which they are expressed.

We must not forget as well that for a patent to be successful, an invention also needs to be novel – that is to say beyond the current *state of the art*. Obviously there is a tension to be drawn here around explaining the proposed invention in detail, including the state of the "*prior art*" and the pitfall of a really great explanation which is so good that it could lead a patent examiner into the fallacy that the invention is in fact obvious!

One of the biggest potential issues in relation to the patenting of "black box" machine learning solutions has to be that of *sufficiency*. If you cannot explain technically how it works, then in order to satisfy the disclosure requirements for a patent (which are that someone unfamiliar with its operation needs to understand how it works) then it may be that you have to disclose the underlying datasets which are used to train it as part of the application.

The final point to note is that several EPO examiners have indicated that using pseudocode and/or UML[106] in an AI patent application – that is to say modelling structures derived from either coding or diagrams, is often far more useful and revealing (particularly in terms of defining the algorithmic "technical effect") than normal language[107].

FRAND Licensing models?

With an increasingly crowded field of registered patents – how free actually are you to create new technologies? This is an increasing concern for the AI industry which is now dominating global patent registrations[108].

The AI market is relatively new and has yet to evolve consistent approaches, however one suggestion has been that it should follow the lead of more mature technological industries and adopt a telecoms style approach which allows for patent pools and FRAND licensing (so called fair, reasonable and non-discriminatory terms).

This type of licensing permits the sharing of complementary patents to develop complex technology (an approach which is adopted in the telecommunications industry for example), and has the societal benefit of improving compatibility for consumers (a particular example in the mobile telecoms space is network interoperability as between the manufacturers of different handsets).

---

[106] Unified Modeling Language

[107] *How to Help an EPO Examiner and Improve Your Odds of Patenting a Computer-Implemented Invention* Gene Quinn, July 21, 2019 – see https://www.ipwatchdog.com/2019/07/21/epo-examiner-patenting-computer-implemented-inventions/id=111061/

[108] A WIPO report published in 2019 (Technology Trends) indicated that Machine Learning is the dominant AI technique and is included now in more than one third of *all* identified inventions.

The Machine as inventor

As we'll see in a moment in relation to Copyright, there is specific provision in the UK Copyright, Designs and Patents Act 1988 (the "CDPA") for the creation of computer generated copyright works – somewhat of a departure from other jurisdictions, such as the United States[109]. What then of the position under Patent law where it is claimed that that the author of an invention is in fact a machine (or that the invention has been created by artificial intelligence?)

This was in fact the position which was alleged in the long running *DABUS* patent cases which were considered by the US, UK and European Patent Offices.

The basic premise of DABUS[110] was that artificial intelligence cannot, at least under current patent laws, be considered to be an inventor. DABUS, itself a creation of a human inventor, Stephen Thaler was alleged to have independently devised two separate inventions, one which was described as beverage container, the other as a fractal light signal for attracting attention. Mr Thaler named DABUS itself as the inventor in the applications which were filed at the respective patent offices. In each case it was essentially determined that an inventor had to be a natural human being[111]. In the UK the decision of the IPO was subsequently affirmed by

---

[109] See for example, and by analogy, the US case of *Naruto (PETA) vs. Slater* 888 F. 3d 418 (9th Cir. 2018), the so called "monkey selfie" case. PETA (People for the Ethical Treatment of Animals) filed a claim against a photographer, David Slater, on the basis that a selfie photograph taken allegedly by Naruto, a macaque monkey was not in fact the property of Slater but was owned by the monkey itself. The US 9th Circuit Court of Appeals ruled that copyright under the US Copyright Act 1976, 17 U.S.C. §§ 101-1332 could not vest in an animal.

[110] *'device for the autonomous bootstrapping of unified sentience'*

[111] USPTO Decision: In re Application of Application No.: 16/524,350: https://www.uspto.gov/sites/default/files/documents/16524350_22apr2020_3.pdf; EPO Decision: https://www.epo.org/news-events/news/2020/20200128.html; UK IPO Decision: https://www.ipo.gov.uk/p-challenge-decision-results/o74119.pdf

the High Court[112].

It seems for the moment at least, that this avenue is closed for patent registration: not a surprise when one considers that the wider debate around machine personality has likewise been shut down. It does however create wider uncertainty about the ability of enterprise to invest in the use of AI when creating patentable IP. This is because a failure to list the correct inventor can open such patents up to challenge and ultimately render them unenforceable.

Copyright

Subject to the above considerations, disembodied software does not (at least within the EU and UK) qualify for patent protection[113] – here we must look to the CDPA which specifically calls out human and machine generated software as capable of protection by copyright[114] provided it meets the required standards of originality. However, it is here that we see some of the logic underpinning software as copyrightable works beginning to break down.

Whilst the CDPA does make provision for computer generated works to be protected by Copyright[115], this still presumes a causal connection (albeit vague) between the relevant acts of the computer and human preparatory work – section 9(3) provides that "*In the case of a literary, dramatic, musical or artistic work which is computer-generated, the author shall be taken to be the person by whom the arrangements necessary for the creation of the work are undertaken.*". The term "*Computer generated*" is defined as

---

[112] [2020] WLD(D)526 see: https://www.bailii.org/ew/cases/EWHC/Patents/2020/2412.html

[113] s1(2)(c) Patents Act 1977 excludes specifically "a scheme, rule or method for performing a mental act, playing a game or doing business, or a program for a computer"

[114] s3(1)(b) Copyright, Designs and Patents Act 1977 specifically includes computer programs as literary works and s12(7) makes explicit provision for works that are generated by Computer, reducing the applicable copyright term to 50 years from the end of the calendar year in which the work was created.

[115] s9(3) Copyright, Designs and Patents Act 1988

follows "*in relation to a work, means that the work is generated by computer in circumstances such that there is no human author of the work.*"[116]. As we have seen, and as I explain further below, machine learning models are increasingly abstracted from human intervention and inherently opaque, and thus, it is argued, the causal connection implied by section 9(3) is becoming increasingly redundant. Indeed the one UK case that has to date been decided in relation to computer generated works – *Nova Productions ltd v. Mazooma Games*[117] applying section 9(3) of the CDPA, provides a highly problematic outcome for the "*learned behaviours*" paradigm I discuss below. Mazooma held that a series of computer generated video game "frames" were either authored directly by the machine or by the person providing arrangements necessary for the creation of the work – in this case, the programmer – and not the *player* of the game. In our current debate, is it not the *trainer* of the machine learning system which is most analogous to the *player*?

As we discovered in Chapter one, the key elements forming a machine learning system are the **Model**, the **Parameters** and the **Learner** which together form the Artificial Neural Network.

The CDPA provides that a literary work "*means any work, other than a dramatic or musical work, which is written, spoken or sung, and accordingly includes…(b) a computer program*" and "*(c) preparatory design material for a computer program*"[118]. It would seem evident in this context that at least the AI **Model** (the logical framework within which the system operates) described above will potentially be eligible for copyright protection. Whilst the CDPA provides no guidance as to originality required for such protection, recital eight of the 2009 Software Directive[119] provides that in determining whether "*a computer program is an original work, no tests as to the qualitative or aesthetic merits of the program should be applied.*" This is to be read in conjunction with Article 1 which provides that "*a computer program shall be protected if it is original in the sense that it is the*

---

[116] s178 Copyright, Designs and Patents Act 1988

[117] [2007] EWCA Civ 219, [2007] Bus LR 1032

[118] s(3)(1) of the Copyright, Designs and Patents Act 1977

[119] Directive 2009/24/EC on the legal protection of computer programs

author's own intellectual creation. No other criteria shall be applied to determine its eligibility for protection."[120]. Clearly the framers of the Directive intended copyright protection to extend merely to the coding aspects of the software concerned and in turn expressly excluded the *outputs* or *products* of that code. Whilst there is no such guidance in the UK CDPA, the Directive should be considered as influential on the approach taken by courts and tribunals within the European Member States.

Obviously at the time the relevant Copyright legislation was framed, software (whether machine or human created) consisted of rigidly programmed linear instruction sets that had no (or at least very limited) ability to adapt and "learn" according to data inputs: the exponential rise in use and development of artificial intelligence has occurred relatively recently.

As we have seen, machine learning systems lack a direct correlation between human input and machine generated output – their models are created within the framework of software but as they are trained or exposed to sufficient amounts of data, their outputs adapt (they are modified by the *Learner* element we discussed in Chapter one, above), and thus they become more adept at solving the application that they are presented with. Machine learning trainers are therefore in a highly influential position to tune and direct system outputs (in this regard I direct the reader back to comments made in relation to the *Mazooma* case).

It is this complex mass of tuned, biased and weighted variables applied progressively to the machine learning model during the training process – in more anthropomorphic terms – "*learned*" or "*trained*" behaviour (discussed further below) – which provides the key difference and arguably the demonstrable and substantial *value* to the users of AI systems. Other than this distinguishing feature there is no underlying difference in the technological hardware and processing platform as between trained and untrained systems. Of course, continuing the anthropomorphic analogy, which is entirely apposite here, the other aspect of learned behaviours is that once they are learned, they cannot be unlearned, and the more relevant learning and experience you are exposed to, the better you

---

[120] See Article 1(3), Directive 2009/24/EC

get at solving a particular problem. This is of particular importance in relation to the large data sets that AI systems are exposed to, especially in circumstances where such data sets are *licensed* for use (implying some form of return of the material so licensed) rather than assigned permanently or owned by the user. We'll consider these two elements of what I have termed the *learned behaviours paradigm* in a moment.

Separately, and distinct from the system itself, there is clearly value in the training data sets that are provided to the relevant machine learning system. This is akin of course to the training materials provided to a child in school education – feed it the right information and hopefully the right outputs will emerge (the child will be properly educated). Don't feed it at all, or feed it the wrong information and what you'll get out of it will also be a waste of time – as the saying goes, *"garbage in, garbage out"*. Curating and assembling training data sets (whether on a supervised or unsupervised basis) is, as we have already mentioned, a critical part in the evolution and development of a useful artificially intelligent system. One has to assume that there will therefore be some not inconsiderable level of skill involved in creating such data sets, and calibrating them to ensure maximal value from a machine learning system.

Algorithms

Algorithms sit at the heart of artificially intelligent systems – clearly the efficiency or otherwise of such algorithms drives the usefulness of such systems – however it is important to note that algorithms *per se* are nothing more than a complex procedural expression or set of rules – a formula.

In the case of machine learning systems, it is algorithms which define at the most fundamental level how the system handles and manages the data inputted into it.

Algorithms fall within a grey area in intellectual property law. When they are expressed as pure mathematical formulae, they are unlikely to be capable of copyright protection as they represent an expression of mathematical fact. However when expressed, encoded and articulated as part of software, they are more likely in principle to enjoy copyright protection.

So far as patent law is concerned, obviously an algorithm represents an idea or concept. As such, the general discussion above on patentability applies. Unless the prior considerations we discussed are followed, they are unlikely to be patentable *per se*. In any event, focussing merely on the protection of the learning or activation algorithms used by an artificially intelligent system (if indeed such are capable of intellectual property protection) solves only one part of the IP jigsaw. An algorithm to a machine learning system is an expression of its most fundamental functions – taking such an approach to the exclusion of the other elements listed in this chapter would be much like attempting to protect the representative chemical synaptic functions of neurons in a human brain whilst excluding its thoughts.

The "learned behaviours" paradigm

Earlier on in this chapter, we described how artificial intelligence systems develop useful learned behaviours over the course of their training process by the refinement of weights, biases and variables within their AI *models* (whether on a supervised, unsupervised or reinforcement basis) and how more comprehensively or effectively trained systems are demonstrably more valuable than their counterparts which although technologically equivalent, have not undergone this process. It is worth recapping the concept of machine learning in order to get a clear picture of what is actually happening inside a machine learning system.

As we saw in Chapter one, what a neural network does when it "*learns*" is apply a series of weights and biases across the successive artificial neuron layers in its network to influence activations within those individual neurons and ultimately the output layer, hopefully achieving the desired correct output. It is ultimately a mathematical process of refinement but a process which leads to optimised and useful output. As noted above, I refer to this for reasons of conceptual ease as "learned behaviour".

We also considered that exposure to training or calibrating sets of data during this training process (and indeed to live production data during normal operational use) could lead to some elements of the data set – principally the associative aspects describing statistical patterns and correlations rather than the content itself – being retained by the machine learning system in an analogous fashion to a taught human being. How then should this paradigm be managed by intellectual property law?

We have seen that copyright will somewhat imperfectly protect the software model or framework within which an artificial intelligence system sits. On the same basis, it might also protect relevant machine learning algorithms but only if they are expressed in a software form. It cannot (in its current guise) protect the output or *learned behaviours* of that system, unless they are expressed in an immutable form in the software construct of the *Model* (as discussed earlier). Immutability however is typically not a characteristic of learned behaviours. As with a human, as a machine learning system is trained and exposed to more data, it becomes better at its assigned task – or in more mechanistic terms, the output becomes further optimised.

Knowhow

Traditionally "*know how*", that is to say the knowledge and knowhow gained by a person experientially and locked up in their heads, is not something that is capable of intellectual property protection. Typically this is because, in human terms, intellectual property protects the *expressions* of ideas rather than the idea itself. Without delving too deeply into the realms of the philosophical, can it be said that the "knowhow" generated by artificially intelligent systems is equivalent?

In practical terms of course, machine learning systems are created by human beings and (for the moment at least) do not share an equivalence with us. They are undoubtedly complex, and we as humans have difficulty understanding on a practical (and even theoretical level) how such systems reach their decisions, but they are still a construct of human endeavour.

Whilst copyright and patent law are unlikely to be of much use in relation to protecting the learned behaviours of trained artificially intelligent systems, it is submitted that in this context there is one intellectual property route that might be extended to protect them, and that is the *trade secret*.

A trade secret is typically a commercially valuable process or item of know-how which has been kept from the public domain.

Traditionally the UK has not had a trade secret regime but has relied on the concept of breach of confidence for protection of such items. Whilst this common law regime provides much equivalence with Trade Secret law, it has traditionally suffered from some conceptual difficulties with the concept of industrial espionage. The United States has long had a trade secret law – see for example the Uniform Trade Secrets Act of 1979 and in this context the EU is perceived as having lagged behind in its intellectual property regime. This has led to the recently published *Directive on the Protection of undisclosed know-how and business information (trade secrets)*[121] or Trade Secrets Directive. The Trade Secrets Directive provides that an item of intellectual property will qualify for protection if: it "*(a) it is secret in the sense that it is not, as a body or in the precise configuration and assembly of its components, generally known among or readily accessible to persons within the circles that normally deal with the kind of information in question; (b) it has commercial value because it is secret; (c) it has been subject to reasonable steps under the circumstances, by the person lawfully in control of the information, to keep it secret*".[122] In the context of our current debate, the learned behaviours (or optimised outputs) of an artificially intelligent system are likely to have been developed through a careful process which will be a combination of training, tuning and exposure to carefully selected training data sets (of which more later). Much of this process is likely to have been developed through experimentation, trial and error and of course considerable investment.

It is likely in the circumstances that the "optimised" machine learning system that results will result in competitive advantage for its owner, and such owner is unlikely to want to voluntarily throw that competitive advantage away by disclosing it to competitors.

Provided the owner has exercised reasonable precautions to keep the process described above away from the public domain, it is plausible that they should be able to claim trade secret protection under the regime proposed by the Trade Secrets Directive. The foregoing should of course be tempered by the fact that there is a very community that will be driven

---

[121] Directive (EU) 2016/943

[122] Trade Secrets Directive Article 1(a),(b) & (c)

by "*open access*" principles to information (see the wider debate on this topic at the end of Chapter three), for the greater good of advancing research into artificial intelligence and there are equally speaking very many open source derived AI algorithms and approaches which obviously will be unlikely to qualify for such intellectual property protection.

Data sets

Custom assembled training data sets (or indeed operational data sets that have been assembled for processing by an AI system) are also, for the reasons articulated above, likely to qualify for similar trade secret style protection.

The informed reader may also wonder about the reach of the Database Directive[123] into this domain – however as that directive is intended to cover a "*scheme of arrangement of data*" (ie a systemically organised database[124]) it is unlikely to be of use in relation to most AI systems whose very power and flexibility comes from their ability to ingest and process multiple items of raw, heterogenous data from different and disparate data sources (sometimes referred to as "data lakes"). Although there are likely to be qualitative decisions made about the types and classes of data to be used for training machine learning systems it is improbable that such data sets would reach the levels of organisation equivalent to a classically ordered database. In the context of neural networks, there may be a role for the Database Directive tangentially in relation to the collective *weights* and *biases* which are applied to individual input neurons in order to influence the network's output (see our earlier discussion on this in the context of Chapter one) – however that analysis appears marginal when one considers that it depends upon these variables being able to be systematically extracted from the operation of the system itself in a useful and repeatable manner.

---

[123] 96/9/EC implemented by the Copyright and Rights in Databases Regulations 1997

[124] Article 1(2) of the Database Directive 96/9/EC provides that "database" means " a collection of independent works, data or other materials arranged in a systematic or methodical way and individually accessible by electronic or other means."

The second part of the learned behaviours paradigm we discussed above was the potential for an AI system to retain associative and relational elements of the data processed by it as part of the training or learning process – such retention enabling improvement in the system's ability to achieve its assigned tasks or in alternate terms, improving its skill level. Conceptually this is difficult to reconcile with traditional intellectual licensing models and data protection law which require the return or destruction of licensed materials at the end of the applicable licensing term or period of use. Irrespective of whether technically such is feasible, as a developer or owner of a machine learning system you are unlikely to want to hand back those associative or relational data elements (so called "*information residuals*") which have improved performance in your system. What this means in practical terms is that any licensing model must take account of these characteristics and either provide for a perpetual license of those data elements which are retained or a full assignment. A failure to do so may render the licensee potentially subject to an action for breach of contract.

Whether this proves to be a substantive issue in the future remains to be seen – practically speaking this is the way in which AI systems function so it would seem to be futile attempting to legislate otherwise. As a practitioner however, you should be aware of this pitfall and provide for appropriate carve outs in any third-party deals which are licensing data sets for machine learning systems.

Infringing and Derivative works

The final part of this chapter is really to flag the ongoing potential for machine learning systems to create infringing and derivative versions of copyrighted works. This is not of itself a new problem – new technologies have enabled a technologically sophisticated environment which empowers the YouTube generation to manipulate video and audio on domestic computers which has in turn driven a culture of plagiarism and derivative works – a perennial problem for major copyright holders. What is new however, and potentially disturbing, is the level of sophistication that AI provides to these users.

"*DeepFake*" software, which is now freely available to computer enthusiasts, enables facial substitution technology in video. Inevitably, this has been driven to the lowest common denominator which has involved pasting the faces of Hollywood "A" list actors into hard core pornography (a course of conduct that could of course give rise to wider defamatory issues) – however it doesn't take much imagination to see this technology being used by fans to paste themselves into their favourite franchises, to substitute or swap preferred actors in movies or even to resurrect long dead actors (something that Hollywood is beginning to dabble in on an "official" basis). Perhaps even more disturbingly given the recent trend of fake news, there are signs that this technology may be used to fake incendiary statements by politicians to fan the flames of extremism and to undermine democratic societies. Indeed California has been at the forefront of attempting to outlaw this use, and passed a State law in October 2019 making such use illegal[125].

In summary we have learned that in the context of artificial intelligence, it is not sufficient to purely rely on the concepts of copyright and patents law – although these still remain fundamentally important, they do not provide one hundred percent coverage and protection for such systems.

Trade secret law also has a part to play in protecting investment in machine learning systems that have been taught, tuned and refined through a process of exposure to carefully curated data sets.

So far as the data sets themselves are concerned, you need to ensure (as owner or developer of a machine learning system) that you allow for *information residuals* to be retained by your system. As a licensor of third party data sets to a machine learning system developer, you should consider how this fact is to be reflected commercially and legally in your licences.

---

[125] See AB730 Deceptive Audio or Visual Media http://leginfo.legislature.ca.gov/faces/billTextClient.xhtml?bill_id=201920200AB730

CHAPTER SIX
AUTOMATED BIAS AND
DISCRIMINATION

One of the very powerful benefits of artificial intelligence when coupled with big data is the ability of such systems to make predictions or synthesise outputs based on the data which have been presented to them. There is an oft quoted popular fallacy which assumes infallibility and impartiality in such systems – in effect that they are immune from bias[126].

The partial truth of course is that whilst machines are generally impervious to human emotion when making decisions –as we shall see in this chapter, this does not necessarily equate to lack of subjectivity in such decisions.

AI systems are very dependent on the quality of the data that is fed into them – they need accurate and representative data sets in order to learn and refine their processing of their assigned application – whether that is on a supervised, unsupervised or reinforcement basis.

Being "*fed*" training data and ongoing operational data is critical to performance improvement and enhancement. This is sometimes referred to as the "*data diet vulnerability*".

A classic example of this (now thankfully rectified) was the original Google Translate algorithm. Rather than being "trained" in a conventional way to follow rules of linguistic grammar, Google Translate acquired its linguistic skills by parsing hundreds of thousands of texts, many of which were centuries old. As you can imagine, the prejudices and cultural stereotypes in those written works ended up being reflected in the translations produced by Google's system. This was particularly problematic in languages with non-specific gender references, as has been particularly well documented – so to take a particular example, if the original

---

126 See the discussion in Chapter three on *automation bias*

version of Google Translate was instructed to translate from English to Turkish and back to English again, the phrase "*HE is lazy*" was translated into "*SHE is lazy*", and the phrase "*SHE is smart*" would be translated to "*HE is smart*".

Clearly Google had to do something about this and they ended up creating a discrimination algorithm to potentially filter these culturally offensive outputs and provide alternatives where the immediate context was equivocal, ultimately a hugely complex task.[127]

The *data diet vulnerability* described above gives rise to another practical legal consideration in relation to the use of machine learning systems – that is the extent to which if such training and operational data sets do contain bias, or are skewed in a particular direction (to e.g. reinforce a specific outcome) they can give rise to automated decisions which are likely to prejudice or discriminate against individuals. In particular it also raises the question of how such bias should be managed at law.

It is an established fact that automating a process – or relegating it to technology can ironically (and somewhat perversely) act to *reduce* oversight in relation to bias thus perpetuating the fallacy of impartiality I describe above.

We are all conditioned to believe in the efficiency of computers. This is clearly a disturbing consideration (and one which should be overtly challenged) where such systems are using data that overtly refers to personally identifiable information. It is especially concerning when one considers that the vulnerability could be deliberately and malevolently exploited in order to make a system biased or discriminatory in addition to the consequences of accidental "*skewing*". Remember also that the breadth of such impact should also be taken into account – consider our earlier discussion on the characteristics of data – discrimination or bias could result from data which indirectly refers to an individual or which is *inferred* or

---

[127] See a very revealing interview with Google's head of translation, Macduff Hughes: https://www.theverge.com/2019/1/30/18195909/google-translate-ai-machine-learning-bias-religion-macduff-hughes-interview

derived from other data.

In addition to the problem of training data sets "hard coding" bias into an artificially intelligent system, there is also the problem of the so-called *"filter bubble"* or *"echo chamber"* effect – which in reality is an extension of the algorithmic bias described above.

Filter bubble effects occur during operational use of AI systems as they learn and adapt outputs to user behaviour – these can act to reinforce or compound bias by serving up decisions and results which are within the data bubble and excluding those which are outside it – even when in some circumstances, the excluded results may be legitimate.

Typically filter bubbles are discussed in the context of intelligent web browsers that try to direct and focus search results based on previous internet browsing behaviour, but the analysis is equally valid in situations where an AI system has learned (through application of data sets) to select or make choices in a distinct manner.

Microsoft's Tay, a bulletin board chatbot launched in 2016, but rapidly and subsequently withdrawn, was a classic example of this. Tay quickly adopted the characteristics of the boards it was posting on and developed overt racist and xenophobic tendencies. It was merely reflecting the unpleasant demographic of the boards it was posting on[128].

Another example which particularly illustrates these problems is in relation to automated recruitment. The recruitment industry has embraced automation wholeheartedly – especially in relation to those jobs which are perceived as commoditised or where the industry must achieve large scale volume recruitment for clients in short timescales. Sectors where there is high demand for interim employment also find such automated approaches attractive. The net result has been a boom in the development of systems that can automate selection and rejection of CVs, right the way through to chatbots or robotic interviewers that can lead discussions and filter candidates.

---

[128] See: https://www.techrepublic.com/article/why-microsofts-tay-ai-bot-went-wrong/

Whilst no one doubts the efficiency of such systems when properly implemented, there are concerns that exclusive dependence on them could, aside from the potential for discrimination and bias described above, lead to recruitment which is based purely on documented skills (via CVs) ignoring softer metrics such as an individual's personality, fit and emotional temperament. A classic example of this was an algorithmic system employed by Amazon to automate recruitment in 2015 (but subsequently quietly withdrawn). It was discovered that the system had taught itself to prefer male candidates over female candidates, allegedly because the relevant models were trained to vet applications over a historic ten-year period – over which time most had been men, reflecting the overwhelmingly traditional male dominance of the technology industry[129]. This is but one example however – there are many instances in modern society where we are increasingly ceding complex decisions to machine learning systems which relate to such diverse matters as the finance we can obtain to the news we read.

The GDPR

So far as the law itself is concerned, it is the General Data Protection Regulation which provides an overarching framework in relation to machine-based decisions. The greatest potential impact for individuals is of course is in relation to those decisions that have *"legal affects that significantly affect data subjects"*[130] – and it is in this context and in the context of profiling[131] which the GDPR attempts to address – see the commentary in Chapter three above.

Clearly automated bias and discrimination was one of the problems that the GDPR was implemented to address. We have already discussed the key principles that apply in these circumstances but it is worth covering generally what the GDPR provides for both in terms of punitive sanctions against controllers and processors that breach the provisions of the

---

[129] See https://www.reuters.com/article/us-amazon-com-jobs-automation-insight-idUSKCN1MK08G

[130] Article 22 – GDPR

[131] Article 4(4) GDPR

regulation and individual remedies for EU citizens who have been unfairly discriminated against – or made the subject of bias.

The GDPR significantly increases the levels of administrative fines that can be levied on data controllers and expands this punitive regime to data processors for the first time. Clearly the amounts of such fines will depend upon the individual circumstances of the particular case and a number of other factors, such as the seriousness of the breach and the extent to which the breach has been repeated[132] but it is evident that European legislators intended the obligations relating to profiling and automated decision making[133] to be subject to an increased level of sanction – up to the higher of 20m or 4% of the total worldwide annual turnover of an undertaking[134].

We have already seen in Chapter three that data controllers which carry out profiling or automated decision making (as defined by Article 22 of the GDPR) can only do so on the basis of the explicit consent of the data subject[135] and that such consent can be withdrawn at any time. Data subjects have additional rights to rectification[136] – including the right to obtain from a data controller without undue delay, the rectification of inaccurate personal data relating to them (in addition to the right to have incomplete or partial data on them completed), as well as a right to erasure (the so called *"right to be forgotten"*)[137]. This is all in addition to a right to direct compensation for data subjects which is enshrined in Article 82 of the Regulation.

It is evident there are a comprehensive suite of remedies and sanctions

---

[132] See Article 83(2)(a)-(k) GDPR for a complete list of qualifying factors

[133] Article 22 GDPR

[134] Article 83(5)(b) GDPR

[135] Article 22(2)(a)-(b) provide for additional carve outs related to the performance of contract obligations and specific authorisations of a Member State, see earlier Chapter three.

[136] Article 16 GDPR

[137] Article 17 GDPR

that are available to counter potential bias and discrimination in relation to processing under the GDPR. However there remains a major concern about identifying whether and how such bias has taken place, which is often very hard to determine, particularly when machine learning technology is involved. Bias and discrimination are key areas which demand further research from machine learning scientists to develop solutions that can audit – or provide a full explanation for – their decisions. As we learned in Chapters one and two the industry is not yet in a position to find convincing technological solutions to provide this explanatory functionality, especially where "*black box*" AI systems are used, although there are clear industry research initiatives to enable it.

The Equality Act 2010

The other potential legal consequences that should be considered in relation to the use of artificially intelligent systems in the UK revolve principally around the Equality Act 2010.

The Equality Act is a consolidating measure in the UK which brings together the former principles set out in predecessor legislation: the Equal Pay Act 1970, the Sex Discrimination Act 1975, the Race Relations Act 1976 and the Disability Discrimination Act 1995, as well as updating the law to provide for age discrimination.

Undoubtedly the Equality Act has a part to play in determining whether or not discrimination has taken place in the workplace and in wider society – its provisions are particularly relevant to the issue of automated bias that are the subject of this chapter. There is a substantial concern however that the law as drafted however does not *explicitly* allow for a right to understand the basis for decisions made by machine learning systems.[138] The Equality Act is frustratingly unclear when it discusses burden of proof in relation to prohibited conduct, particularly when considering the nature and circumstances of algorithmic selection and decision making by artificially intelligent systems which (as we have already dis-

---

[138] See for example the report of the Future of Work Commission, December 2017 (commissioned by the Labour Party)

cussed in the context of Chapter two above) do not directly translate human actions into machine outputs. Section 136 of the Act for example provides that "*If there are facts from which the court would decide, in the absence of any other explanation, that person (A) contravened the provision concerned, the court must hold that the contravention occurred.*"[139]. Generally Section 136 dictates an absolutist and relatively unsubtle approach – it does not really address concerns about AI transparency – the use of automated machine learning tools to make opaque selection decisions which could potentially be discriminatory and where direct human intervention in such decisions may be limited.

Until this position is clarified, we are in the awkward position of relying on the general rights we have described above under the GDPR and extrapolating the Equality Act's current drafting into our immediate context to see how it might apply. As before, our discussion is based on an analysis of the use of machine learning technologies in this context and I do not propose to provide a comprehensive summary of the Act.

What we are concerned about here is the potential for an AI system that is responsible for decision making, choices and selection to directly or indirectly discriminate against an individual's "*protected characteristics*", as these are defined through the introduction of bias in training or operational data. We have already established the potential for such machine learning systems to make decisions which due to the complexity of their processing capabilities can be incredibly difficult to rationalise on a human explicable basis and also that the learned behaviours they exhibit can "*skew*" decisions in a particular direction (the so-called *filter bubble* effect we discussed earlier).

The Equality Act itself creates a number of obligations which can lead to civil and potential criminal consequences. Criminal causation and artificial intelligence is a topic we consider specifically in Chapter six – which should be reviewed if you are interested in a more in-depth analysis of machine commissioned offences. So far as this chapter is concerned, we'll consider the prohibited acts contemplated by the Act and the provisions

---

[139] s136 (2)

of Schedule 25[140], which provide some indirect pointers as to what types of machine processing are specifically excluded from its provisions.

The Equality Act makes the following *"protected characteristics"* – age[141], disability[142], gender reassignment[143], marriage and civil partnership[144], race[145], religion or belief[146], sex[147] and sexual orientation[148]. It then specifies several types of prohibited conduct in relation to those protected characteristics, which fall within Direct Discrimination[149] – being treated less favourably directly or overtly on the basis of possessing one of these protected characteristics (for example being denied a promotion on the basis of homosexuality) and Indirect Discrimination[150] – often unintended, where a provision, criterion or practice is applied equally to a group but which will ostensibly have the indirect effect of putting those who have the protected characteristic at a disadvantage.

Indirect discrimination is probably the most concerning from the perspective of machine learning given our description above, in that it is the situation which is most likely to occur when a generalised algorithmic approach is applied to a class of people. This is conduct which appears neutral but when applied to someone with a protected characteristic puts

---

[140] Information Society Service Providers

[141] s5

[142] s6

[143] s7

[144] s8

[145] s9

[146] s10

[147] s11

[148] s12

[149] s13

[150] s19

them at a disadvantage. It is also worth mentioning that there are additional prohibited acts relating to Harassment[151] (unwanted conduct by someone against another (or overtly sexual conduct) which degrades the victim or creates a humiliating or offensive situation) and perhaps less relevant to this discussion, Victimisation[152] (essentially detrimental treatment triggered by 'whistleblowing').

The Act applies to those parties carrying out the prohibited conduct (generally in an employment context, this will be an employer) but in addition also applies to "*service providers*". Service Providers are defined as those " ...*concerned with the provision of a service to the public or a section of the public (for payment or not)*"[153].

It is important to note that a service provider for the purposes of the Act may not necessarily correspond with an AI provider in the narrow sense that we are discussing for the purposes of this chapter, but equally speaking *might*.

Service providers under the Equality Act provide any service. So for example when in 2015 a female paediatrician was allegedly unable to access the female changing rooms at her gym (because the automated swipe card system had incorrectly correlated the title "Dr" to exclusively male members), the Gym provider (the service provider) could have been liable for directly discriminating against her on the basis of her sex[154].

The provider of an AI system could conceivably be a service provider for the purposes of the Equality Act if offering a service directly to the public. In a non-public context (for example, where an employer has licensed the use of a machine learning system as a tool for use within its own business), it seems likely that employers will also be fixed with liability for the consequences of their machine learning systems in addition to any potential

---

[151] s26

[152] s27

[153] s29

[154] https://www.dailymail.co.uk/news/article-3000705/Female-paediatrician-locked-gym-changing-room-computer-assumed-Doctor-title-MAN.html

liability which the AI provider might also accrue. Section 109(2) of the Equality Act provides that "*Anything done by an agent for a principal, with the authority of the principal, must be treated as **also** being done by the principal*" (emphasis added).

For the purposes of the Act, there is an important liability distinction as between service providers and employers in that whilst employers have a defence to a claim for discrimination on the basis that they take all reasonable steps to prevent it from arising[155], service providers are automatically fixed with the consequences of using technology. In practical terms this means of course that such service providers should consider very carefully the use of such technology in the provision of their service. As we have already seen, given the very complex nature of artificially intelligent systems it would be prudent in such circumstances for guarantees to be obtained from the machine learning provider that there are no instances of inbuilt bias or prejudice in their system and if and to the extent such does occur, contractual remedies, such as indemnities and other financial recompense, should be available.

Service providers may avoid liability under the Equality Act if they fall within the definition of "*Information Society Service Providers*" under Schedule 25, but in practical terms it seems clear that any utility of this provision to artificial intelligence providers is vanishingly slight.

Information Society Services are defined by the UK E-Commerce regulations[156] as "*any service normally provided for remuneration at a distance, by means of electronic equipment for the processing (including digital compression) and storage of data, at the individual request of a recipient of the service.*" Obviously the provisions of the Equality Act and the E-Commerce regulations were drafted before the advent of meaningful developments in artificial intelligence and machine learning. Some machine learning solutions will not fall within this definition, but it is conceivable that a subscription based machine learning service might. At the time

---

[155] s109(4)

[156] Electronic Commerce (EC Directive) Regulations 2002 implementing the EU Electronic Commerce Directive 2002, repeated in Schedule 25 paragraph 7 (1) (2) (b)

Schedule 25 was intended to ensure that most online businesses within the EU were excluded from the operation of the Equality Act to the extent they were acting as a *"mere conduit"*[157] – providing access to a communications network or transmission within a communication network of information; a *"cache"*[158] – providing a temporary storage facility purely to facilitate the onwards transmission of information or a *"host"*[159] – storing information provided by a recipient of the service.

Crucially for the purposes of our analysis, Schedule 25 exemptions are removed in the case of conduits *"if the information is stored for longer than is reasonably necessary for the transmission"*[160] and in the case of caching if the service provider *"does not modify the information"*[161], both conditions of which it seems likely would be transgressed by the provider of a typical AI system.

So what are the remedies that are available to individuals that have been discriminated against? UK Tribunals and courts have various powers available to them, the most significant of which is that they can award compensation for both financial losses and what are termed "injury to feelings" awards. Such bodies can also make declarations and recommendations.

Compensation can technically be awarded against both a company and an individual perpetrator, although in the case of automated/AI decisions, this is obviously likely to be less relevant. *Injury to feelings* damages are awarded on what is known as the Vento scale[162]. This generally prescribes three "bands" – the lower band, which applies to less serious cases where the act of discrimination is a one off or isolated occurrence; the

---

[157] Paragraph 3, Schedule 25 EA 2010

[158] Paragraph 4, Schedule 25 EA 2010

[159] Paragraph 5, Schedule 25 EA 2010

[160] Paragraph 3 (4), Schedule 25

[161] Paragraph 4 (3) (a), Schedule 25

[162] Named after *Vento v. Chief Constable of West Yorkshire Police* [2002] EWCA Civ 1871 which established the principles

middle band which applies to serious cases that do not fall within the higher band; and the higher band which applies in the most serious cases, for example where there has been a lengthy campaign of discrimination and/or harrassment. Typically in most service provision cases, the tendency has been to award such damages in in the lower band, as such cases of discrimination tend to be one off, isolated incidents.

"Fake News" and other data biases

The foregoing sections of this chapter cover laws on discrimination generally – assessing liability for the users of AI systems that make decisions which have *real* and significant consequences for *real* people. One should not however underestimate the potential for machine learning to continue to permeate within and influence other aspects of our lives less directly and in doing so the corresponding potential for it to spread "*data bias*" as well.

One particular example springs to mind – new digital media is a specific case in point where the assembly of "custom" news items can lead to the filter bubble effect we described above. In more extreme cases there is the potential for ill-intentioned state actors to influence media content by so called "fake news" – indeed there continues to be much publicity to this effect in relation to the US presidential election of 2020.

Artificially intelligent machines are taking increasing responsibility for actually writing and assembling "news" or social media items automatically and are capable of expertly manipulating photo-realistic images with no noticeable artefacts. As we saw in Chapter five, this has been taken to extreme lengths recently through the creation of machine learning neural network software that can be trained to substitute one face for another in a segment of video – so called "*deep fakes*", some of which are extremely convincing and latterly disturbing.

CHAPTER SEVEN
AI CRIME: COMMISSION AND JUDGMENT

We look at two aspects of criminal liability in this chapter. The first is to examine the realistic potential for artificially intelligent systems to be liable under criminal law for the commission of an offence. The second, and I suspect rather less theoretical question, is to examine the extent to which artificial intelligence systems are influencing sentencing and bail decisions made in relation to those within the criminal justice system.

In Chapter two we looked at the legal theory of causation in a civil context – principally through the filters of tort, contract and product liability. Criminal causation is inevitably and inexorably linked to this discussion. Necessarily our debate will touch on robots in addition to artificial intelligence. As we discovered in Chapter one, modern day robots may share some characteristics with disembodied machine learning systems if they have enabled machine learning software elements – the additional factor of course is that they interact *physically* with the real world which gives them the potential to undertake *physical* acts which could lead to criminal consequences in the real world.

Pure machine learning systems in contrast are constrained by digital barriers in relation to the criminal consequences they could potentially create, although given current cybercrime levels this does not make an analysis of such systems in this context any less relevant, particularly so as those digital barriers become more permeable and connectivity between systems and smart-functionality becomes more and more ubiquitous.

Crimes at their most basic interpretation are of course acts which are deemed – either through the application of common law or by statute – as abhorrent or contrary to the normal functioning of society, the commission of which brings about a punitive consequence. Taking aside strict liability offences, there are three basic prerequisites for criminal liability to be established in human actors – the *Actus Reus* – or criminal act; the

Mens Rea – or criminal intent (the so called guilty mind), and *concurrence* or *coincidence* – the coincidence of both of the former. Liability cannot be established generally unless the actor has a guilty mind and in tandem perpetrates the criminal deed.

The Actus Reas element as we know can be expressed by acts or omissions and the Mens Rea element has various levels ranging from knowledge and specific intent all the way to criminal negligence or "recklessness".

So far as machine-based liability itself is concerned, there are essentially three models which have been debated by commentators and bear analysis – the first does not impute any special characteristics to the AI system.

Instrumental extension

The "*instrumental extension*" model treats AI as a tool or instrumental extension of the perpetrator, which is where the real criminal liability is focussed. This model works well, as in civil causation, where the actions of the machine are directly attributable to the actions of its user. Conventional computers, and indeed most inanimate objects, are particularly suited to this linear causality. Take for example the scenario of an entirely "dumb" factory robot, which through the direct controlled actions of its user, manages to kill a factory worker. The robot here has direct equivalence with a knife or a gun. Provided the user has the requisite *mens rea*, it seems likely that the elements of murder will be established.

The requirement of concurrence has also evolved in English jurisprudence to cover not just temporal concurrence but also motivational concurrence – provided that the guilty actor has the motivation to carry out the crime, it is not necessary for the *actus reus* to coincide in time. Many crimes are in fact the product of a sequence of connected events leading to the commission of an offence[163]. Taking our earlier example of a "dumb" robot, it seems likely therefore that even if our user had programmed the robot *earlier* to behave in a particular way likely to cause the death of the factory worker (in the full knowledge that the factory

---

[163] See for example *R v. Le Brun [1991] CA*; *R v. Jakeman (1982) CA*; *Fagan v. Metropolitan Police Commissioner [1968] QBD*

worker would be present at that time) he would not escape criminal liability.

Machine Learning systems however are one step removed from this. As we have seen, they are not directly programmed but rather trained, over a period of time, in relation to a particular task. As we discussed in Chapter one, their learning can be influenced by appropriate data sets but their behaviours (or outputs) are not directed by prescriptive programmed instructions. By their very nature, many such systems are inherently opaque. There are of course likely to be examples of criminality where this disconnection will be problematic from an evidential point of view – especially if for example, the object of the criminal actors is to use machine learning tools to obfuscate or hide their criminal activities and more specifically (and problematically) their criminal *intent* – e.g. in a complex money laundering case (in this regard it is important to remember the distinction between burdens of proof in criminal cases and civil ones – whereas a civil case need be proved only on a *balance of probabilities*, the evidential burden in criminal cases is much higher – *beyond reasonable doubt*).

In other cases however, this disconnect is likely to be relatively meaningless given the context and circumstances – take the recent 2015 case (publicised somewhat melodramatically in the media as "*Robot gets arrested*") of a Swiss art collective that used an intelligent "bot" armed with $100 worth of bitcoin to purchase Ecstasy tablets, a Hungarian Passport and various spying devices as part of an art installation on the power of the so called "Dark Web". The system (called "*Random Dark Net Shopper*") purchased the items and had them delivered to the art gallery – a relatively easy way to track down the perpetrators.[164]

Natural and probable consequences

The next model which has been proposed in the context of machine liability is what is termed the "*natural probable consequences*" model. I should say at the outset that this is a highly problematic doctrine in its

---

[164] See Guardian dated 22 April 2015 "*Swiss Police release robot that bought ecstasy online*"

own right and has been largely discredited in many US states, as well as comparable jurisdictions, such as the UK which expressly prohibited its application by s8 of the Criminal Justice Act 1967[165].

In this model, the AI system takes action which is a "*natural and probable*" consequence of its training. So going back to our earlier example of the robot killing a factory worker, (assuming our machine now has artificial intelligence capabilities), in this model, the creator of the artificially intelligent system does not need to have a specific intent (or *mens rea*) to kill the factory worker, but rather a state of criminal negligence – that is to say reckless disregard as to whether the training of the machine learning system could lead to the death of the factory worker – if a reasonable person in the place of the creator could have forseen the offence as a *natural probable consequence* of the way in which the process was conducted. The doctrine evolved as a way to embrace accomplice liability (i.e. where there been offence committed by an accomplice which is not part of a conspiracy, but which would otherwise be a "natural probable consequence" of a criminal scheme) and essentially side steps the subjective requirement for juries to assess whether or not the guilty party possessed the necessary mens rea. Ironically, given the difficulties we have discussed above in relation to the opaque way in which machine learning systems operate, this doctrine (although effectively discredited) might in fact provide a more convenient route for the judicial system to establish appropriate criminal liability in cases where artificially intelligent systems have been used in the commission of an offence.

Direct machine liability

Finally, there is the theoretical possibility of a criminal liability model which assumes some level of responsibility *per se* on the part of the machine for its actions. I refer to theoretical because, as we have learned, liability and accountability both require some element of understanding and self-awareness on the part of the artificially intelligent system for the

---

[165] s8 of the 1967 Act reversed the position reached in *DPP v. Smith (1961) AC 290* which originally proposed a "natural and probable consequences" test as a means to attempt to objectively translate criminal recklessness into intent

consequences of its actions.

To a certain degree this plays back to our debate on individuation in the context of civil causation in Chapter two. Despite the views of many populist commentators, we are not currently at a technological state of the art where this is relevant.

How then should the criminal justice system respond to increasingly complex crimes in which increasingly complex machines play significant parts? The response must logically be dictated in a similar manner to the conclusions I reach in Chapter two – if the natural and probable consequence doctrine cannot be reinvigorated in criminal situations where machine intelligence is deployed, potentially making the issue of determining whether the alleged defendants to a crime have the requisite *mens rea,* then the response of the legislators has to be to consider an increase in the scope of strict liability offences.

Strict liability

Generally strict liability offences are those under which intention does not have to be proven in relation to an aspect of the *actus reus,* although some element of intent may be required in relation to the other aspects of the offence in question – such as recklessness. Strict liability offences are as a rule created by Statute – however typically, Parliament does not make it expressly clear in most instances whether an offence should be one of strict liability. Indeed this may be an unintended consequence of some Acts which are poorly drafted or vague in their approach.

The courts apply several principles to override the general presumption of *mens rea* to establish strict liability[166]. For the purposes of our current analysis, it makes sense to focus on these principles which are likely to come into sharp focus in circumstances where use of intelligent machines cause injury or loss, and that is where a statutory offence is dealing with an issue of social concern.

---

[166] In *B (a minor) v. DPP (2000)*

The leading case of *Gammon (Hong Kong) v. AG*[167] provides that where a statute is legislating on an issue of social concern, and the creation of strict liability will promote the purpose of the statute by encouraging individuals to take extra measures against committing the offence, the general presumption in favour of mens rea can be rebutted.

Typically the courts will not make this leap where the offence is a "real" crime with moral consequences as opposed to an offence which is regulatory in nature[168] (usually one where no moral issues are involved) or one which carries serious penalties – generally they are more willing to do so in cases where the penalties for breach are relatively small – but this is not a rule which is applied prescriptively.

The Gammon case concerned a failure on the part of the defendants to follow building plans accurately (due to the imposition of changes) which caused a major building collapse in Hong Kong. Under the relevant building and construction regulations there was a maximum penalty for breach of up to three years in prison or a fine of $250,000. The Privy Council upheld the view that the offence was one of strict liability and it did not matter whether the defendants were aware that their changes may have led to the collapse.

As the use of artificially intelligent systems becomes more pervasive in society, so inevitably the tendency of the clever and ill-intentioned to avoid criminal sanctions will increase commensurately and of course in many clever, convoluted and devious ways that cannot be predicted. The extension of strict liability could provide society with an organic and flexible response to these changing circumstances which do not necessitate a wholesale change to the way in which we judge criminal accountability.

The criminal justice system – bail and sentencing decisions

The second part of this chapter takes a look at the increasing use of machine learning systems in the criminal justice system – specifically in relation to the sentencing of crimes. The increased uptake of such systems

---

[167] [1985] AC 1

[168] See *Sweet v. Parsley [1970] AC 132*

raises the spectres of bias, discrimination and accountability (and the increased potential for claims which are based on the misuse of such systems) which we have discussed in previous chapters but which it is important to discuss in the context of crime.

In the criminal justice system, artificial intelligence is now being used in the United States and the United Kingdom to make sentencing, bail and parole decisions for prisoners. The US criminal case of *State v. Loomis*[169], provides a somewhat worrying example of the rise of such technology (and the court's attitude to its use). Eric Loomis was charged in early 2015 with five criminal counts in a drive by shooting in Wisconsin. In the event, the defendant pleaded guilty to two lesser of the five charges. In preparation for his sentencing hearing, the Wisconsin Department of Corrections produced a pre-sentencing investigation report (a so called "PSI"), that included an AI assessment of his potential to commit further crime.

The system used in Loomis' assessment was COMPAS, developed by Equivant. COMPAS is a decision tree-based classification solution and uses interviews with offenders as well as information from their criminal records history to determine the risk of recidivism. As such it is employed primarily in the US criminal justice system to assess eligibility for parole, bail and also to determine sentencing levels.

Ironically, given the nature of the algorithmic solution, which is more white box than black box (see our discussion at Chapter one), both Loomis and the Court were prevented from obtaining details as to how the system had classified him for sentencing on the basis that the methodology the system used was proprietary in nature – specifically a trade secret.

The Wisconsin Supreme Court found that the defendant's due process had not been violated by use of an algorithmic sentencing system, even though it was not made clear to the defendant or the court *how* it had reached the conclusions it had in his particular case. Instead, the court ruled that any future use of such automated assessments needed to be

---

[169] 881 N.W. 2d 749 (Wis. 2016)

subject to notification of certain "health warnings". These health warnings should be directed to the court reviewing the system's decisions in any particular situation in order to prevent blind acceptance of its findings and to introduce a degree of judicial scepticism. Whilst this approach clearly acknowledges the risk of relying on algorithmic risk assessment, it provided cold comfort for the defendant in the Loomis case. It is particularly interesting to note that this case is unlikely to have been decided in an equivalent manner in the EU – even if perhaps the outcome of the case might have been the same.

Article 22 of the GDPR on Automated Decision making and profiling prevents (as we have seen previously in Chapter three) cursory human involvement in such decision making and would require active and participative involvement in the part of the judges involved when making a sentencing decision.

CHAPTER EIGHT
MARKET DISTORTING EFFECTS:
AI AND COMPETITION LAW

Competition and trade sit at the heart of western democratic societies. The fundamental principles enshrined in the European Union's 1958 Treaty of Rome – now the "*TFEU*" or "*Treaty on the functioning of the EU*" have as their bases the general aspiration that within the European Union, trade should be unfettered and that goods and services be allowed to develop market equilibrium free of behaviours such as organised *cartels* (companies coming together in a concerted fashion to maintain or fix prices or share markets or customers or otherwise distort market forces) or the *abuse of a dominant market position* (using a monopoly position to exploit customers or to entrench that monopoly).

Again, I do not propose within this chapter to provide a comprehensive guide to competition law (there are other more detailed texts which achieve this aim), but rather to contextualise our debate on machine learning within the framework of competition law rules and provide you the reader with an appreciation of the issues which might apply when using AI tools in this setting.

Competition law is a public interest driven exception to the principle of freedom of contract. Effective competition typically drives lower prices, better quality and choice and more innovation, so it is in the public – (ie. the consumer's) interest that companies do not co-operate or collude in ways which impede the free play of those market forces of competition.

Powerful machine learning tools can be deployed to increase the individual economic efficiency of undertakings. Reducing your cost base is a pro-competitive move which (absent dominance), competition law will not interfere with. But if such tools are used in a co-ordinated way, or if the agreement between the business and the AI supplier contains restrictions on competition (such as, for example, exclusivity provisions or "*most favoured customer*" clauses, then there may be regulatory tension in relation to the permissible use of such tools in an economic context.

Article 101(1) TFEU[170] provides that "*The following shall be prohibited as incompatible with the internal market: all agreements between undertakings, decisions by associations of undertakings and concerted practices which may affect trade between Member States and which have as their object or effect the prevention, restriction or distortion of competition…and in particular those which: (a) directly or indirectly fix purchase or selling prices…; (b) limit or control production, markets, technical development, or investment; (c) share markets or sources of supply;* [and/or] *(d) apply dissimilar conditions to equivalent transactions with other trading parties, thereby placing them at a competitive disadvantage; (e)… ".* Article 101(3) provides for the derogation to this overarching principle (where the agreement, decision or concerted practice of undertakings may be allowed) if it "*contributes to improving the production or distribution of goods or to promoting technical or economic progress, while allowing consumers a fair share of the resulting benefit*" and does not either impose unnecessary restrictions (ie. those indispensable to the objectives expressed in Article 101(3))[171] or provide such undertakings with the possibility of "*eliminating competition*" for a substantial part of the products in question[172]. Article 102 TFEU then goes on to explain the European Union position on abuses of a dominant market position: "*Any abuse by one or more undertakings of a dominant position within the internal market … shall be prohibited as incompatible with the internal market in so far as it may affect trade between Member States. Such abuse may, in particular, consist in: (a) directly or indirectly imposing unfair purchase or selling prices or other unfair trading conditions; (b) limiting production, markets or technical development to the prejudice of consumers;* [and/or] *(c) applying dissimilar conditions to equivalent transactions with other trading parties, thereby placing them at a competitive disadvantage; (d) ….".* There are derogations from these overarching principles (such as for example in relation to agricultural trade between the EU Member States – protecting the Common Agricultural Policy; in relation to the Defence industry; and finally intellectual property licensing), but I do not propose

---

[170] Post-Brexit, much of the EU competition law regime has effectively been 'mirrored' in English law, see Chapters I and II of the Competition Act 1998 as amended by the Competition (Amendment etc.) (EU Exit) Regulations 2019, SI 2019 No. 93

[171] See Article 101(3)(a) TFEU

[172] See Article 101(3)(B) TFEU

to dwell on these here. Additionally, the United States has similar, but not precisely equivalent provisions in its anti-trust legislation, predominantly enshrined in the Sherman Act[173].

The essential question to understand for the purposes of this text is to understand how the use of machine learning tools can undermine these central principles and if so, in what manner. The essence of our debate in this context has similarities with, and draws from, our previous discussions in relation to bias and discrimination (Chapter five) and big data (Chapter three). Put simply, machine learning systems have the ability to analyse and correlate hugely complex pools of data and review dimensionalities in such data which are far beyond what could be achieved by humans in any realistic timeline.

As we move completely into digital data processing and away from an essentially analog documentary existence, vast amounts of data have become available to information processing systems. It is not just the ability to spot patterns at a superhuman level which is interesting from a competition law perspective, but also the ability of such systems to make autonomous decisions and react on the basis of such data almost instantaneously.

Pro-competitive vs. anti-competitive effects

The impact of machine learning on anti-trust and competition principles creates a uniquely polarised duality, and one which is highly market specific. One of the best ways to illustrate this and to show how such technologies can act potentially both as a competition enabler and blocker is to look at an industry specific contextual example.

As we saw in Chapter three, in the context of our discussion on big data, the insurance industry has been one of the trailblazers for use of machine learning technology. Artificial intelligence is rapidly transforming the way in which insurance is priced, quoted for and underwritten. Increasing sophistication is allowing new insurance intermediary start-ups to model synthetic claims data to enable much more accurate pricing of risk.

---

[173] See sections 1 and 2 of the Sherman Act 1890

As these intermediaries gather more and more actual claims data (and more insurers participate in these intermediary platforms), their machine learning solutions become ever more accurate. The competitive impact of such tools depends upon who is deploying them: access to smaller underwriters may enable them to compete more efficiently in the market – effectively levelling the playing field, whilst price competition between the larger players may reduce if multiple parties use the same algorithmic pricing output.

In many situations the availability of online tools, such as price aggregation services and online commerce platforms drive healthy competition by forcing the market to respond in a number of ways: by for example, increasing pricing transparency and creating new routes to market for smaller businesses, reducing barriers to entry in a marketplace. To take a particular example if (ignoring for the moment the numerous regulatory hurdles involved) you have a mobile phone and a car, you can now compete with a taxi driver through driving apps such as Uber.

Product and service aggregation sites can act to facilitate competition by providing consumers with more easily accessible choice (indeed in some markets we now have aggregators that sit over multiple other aggregators to further enhance choice and price, such as SkyScanner[174], which essentially "sweeps" price aggregation data for airline tickets and flights from other aggregators). Finally, artificial intelligence is fuelling an increasingly dynamic environment where pricing for goods and services can be adjusted in accordance with a number of complex external supply and demand factors – both actual and now predicted, on a near instantaneous basis to ensure that the most competitive pricing is offered in a way that would be inconceivable in a predominantly physical (*"bricks and mortar"*) environment.

This essentially pro-competitive and beneficial view of digital competitive trends is however qualified by the reality of many competitive marketplaces which are dominated by a single monopolistic, or a few large oligopolistic, players. Businesses such as Google have seen significant fines for behaviour which the European Commission judges to be anti-

---

[174] See www.skyscanner.net

competitive and damaging to its customers and/or the structure of competition.

Companies are increasingly realising that algorithms and big data are the fuel that drives their businesses and the key which will enable them to unlock more business and outperform their competitors. In many areas of modern business therefore it is as much about a race to obtain and secure large amounts of data in relation to the consumers of your products and services as it is about identifying pricing trends in those items.

Artificially intelligent systems put data acquisition and data manipulation on another, higher, much more sophisticated plane – not only can they analyse data as I have already described, but now they can also apply analytics to synthesise or predict data (as we saw in the context of Chapter three above) which will determine pricing, availability, demand trends and other likely contextual information about the goods and services in question. Indeed, algorithmic systems are now being used to "*micro target*" consumers so that it is possible that you will be offered different pricing (when compared to another consumer) for the same service or product based on your perceived demand for it or some other characteristic, such as where you live, or be offered complementary products to those you have actually purchased.

Consider as well that much of this sophistication is offered within "*walled-garden*" ecosystems that have been developed by companies such as Amazon and eBay which have become so powerful that they cannot be ignored by other retailers (who in consequence, have to join them) and rather than enhanced competition, what might be happening is a recipe for consumers to have their choices limited either because they become bound to a single dominant marketplace or in the alternative are limited to using a few dominant players in an oligopoly.

In each case listed above there is in fact limited or no effective price competition – either because in the former, the *walled garden* can ultimately determine its own price equilibrium, which could potentially signal price monopolisation or in the latter where our oligopolistic players reach price stabilisation (or *harmonised* prices), not through any overt collusive activity, but simply because the algorithmic systems used by them have reached the same conclusion – in competition terms, through a process of *unconscious parallelism*.

These are of course polarised examples of the potential market effects of AI on economic activity – the world is a messy place and in reality the effect of artificial intelligence systems on trade and competition will need to be assessed on the facts of the individual case. We have not yet reached a unity in the deployment of artificial intelligence systems or indeed in terms of utilised data sets – as we have seen there are a variety of technological solutions being continuously developed and enhanced, and the reality is that different businesses gain different advantages from the use of these new tools. Such price and cost asymmetries will aid in the maintenance of a healthily competitive market. On the other hand, we cannot ignore the fact that in many markets the cost of entry is increasingly being driven by big data acquisition which, of itself, could prove a much higher barrier.

One of the biggest issues for anti-trust regulators in this context will of course be to spot and identify potentially insidious *automated* anti-competitive behaviours as we increasingly move into a digitalised environment.

Since the publication of the last edition of this book, it would not be an exaggeration to state that there has been an exponential increase in the use of machine learning in the trade and retail sectors. This has been accompanied by corresponding degrees of enhanced sophistication in the application of questionable manipulative techniques, many of which are complex and difficult from a regulatory perspective to analyse and track. It is worth spending some time analysing a selection of these techniques and behaviours and then examining what the appropriate regulatory responses have been to date.

Dark Patterns

This term, specifically referenced in a 2019 paper[175] but initially coined by UX designer Harry Brignull in 2010, refer to the interface designs created by online services that are created to steer or deceive users psychologically into making unintended and potentially harmful decisions, or rather more bluntly *"tricks used in websites and apps that make you buy or sign up for things that you didn't mean to"*[176].

Dark patterns exploit human behaviours in incredibly subtle ways. They are therefore particularly difficult in isolation to pinpoint as potentially anti-competitive behaviours but combined can have significant impact on online retail performance. There are countless examples of dark patterns, such as burying critical functions which may harm the on-line service – Brignull's so called *"Roach Motel"* technique[177], to use of faked blotches, hairs or marks on banners to induce users of touchscreen enabled devices to touch and hence click on them. Algorithmic interference can enhance these techniques, for example by amplifying scarcity messages on hotel websites to encourage impulse booking, or providing misleading price comparisons between hotels, such as those posted on sites such as Trivago, which itself has been the subject of a competition investigation and subsequent legal proceedings by the Australian Competition and Consumer Commission for misleading consumers[178].

---

[175] *Dark Patterns at scale: Findings from a crawl of 11K shopping websites* Proc. ACM Hum.-Comput. Interact., Vol. 3, No. CSCW, Article 81

[176] Brignull – see www.darkpatterns.org

[177] a particular example of this would be the way in which Amazon hides its "account closure" function, burying it in an obscure part of the website (not related to the "my account" section) taking seven embedded website clicks to reach, followed by an automated webchat – See *How Dark Patterns Trick You Online*, YouTube video by Nerdwriter1

[178] The ACCC's complaints were upheld by the Australian Federal Court in *ACCC v Trivago N.V. [2020] FCA 16* (20 January 2020)

Discrimination by Algorithm

Of course the flip side to the beneficent *"micro-targeting"* practices we discuss above is the potential for algorithms to facilitate unlawful discrimination against consumers, to potentially exclude consumers or deprive them from optimal pricing, or other digitally provided services whether directly and overtly or inadvertently. This concept is discussed at length in Chapter six on bias.

Self-Preferencing

Self-preferencing refers to the exclusionary and/or self-benefiting techniques adopted by the so-called *"walled garden"* markets we discuss above to favour their own products at the expense of competitive ones from third parties. The *Google Shopping* case[179] is an extreme case illustrating the practice. By selective application of its own ranking algorithms, Google was found to have given its own comparison shopping service preferential treatment over competitor services in its general search results pages and consequently to have infringed EU competition law.

Regulatory Responses

Competition and anti-trust law has a long history both in Europe and the United States – certainly reaching back before the advent of digital computers.

Some argue that Competition authorities are increasingly becoming less capable of taking on anti-competitive behaviours which will ultimately harm consumers because economic activity is transitioning away from the human physical medium towards a digital environment which takes place within and between autonomous machines. We have already examined the potential duality of impact of these technologies in relation to competition and anti-trust principles, which inevitably is highly dependent on context.

What to date then has the response been of the Competition authorities

---

[179] EU Case AT.39740, 27th June 2017

to the use of these technologies?

Since the first edition of this book, there is increasing evidence that regulators have developed and deepened their understanding of anti-competitive machine learning led behaviours and are themselves approaching these issues with higher degrees of sophistication. I wrote in 2018 on an OECD consultation document that was published in mid-2017 on the threats posed by algorithmic collusion[180], and the responses of various international regulators which were less than insightful. Since then, the UK Competition and Markets Authority has launched a consultation on Algorithmic Harm[181] which is discussed in Chapter twelve.

In the US, the FTC has shown an increasingly proactive willingness to involve itself in wide-ranging AI policing on a trade and consumer related basis generally, in a similar manner to the privacy and data protection focus adopted by regulators within the EU and UK[182].

The FTC assumes responsibility for this wider role as part of its remit under the Fair Credit Reporting Act (FCRA) 1970 and the Equal Credit Opportunity Act (ECOA) 1974 which both address automated decision making. The FTC Act itself prohibits unfair and deceptive practices causing loss to consumers arising from the use of AI. The FTC's own guidance in this space provides that the use of AI should be transparent, fair and empirically sound, while fostering accountability.[183]

The position however on officially reported cases remains essentially the same: there has been a paucity of officially reported cases considering the effect of machine learning in a competition scenario. In the UK the com-

---

[180] Algorithms and Collusion – Summaries of Contributions, OECD 21-23 June 2017, DAF/COMP/WD(2017) 2

[181] Algorithms: How they can reduce competition and harm consumers, 19th January 2021

[182] See the discussion in Chapter four on the Everalbum case

[183] See *Using Artificial Intelligence and Algorithms* https://www.ftc.gov/news-events/blogs/business-blog/2020/04/using-artificial-intelligence-algorithms

petition authorities have considered a case where price matching algorithms were used to implement a cartel between Amazon marketplace competitors, but no cases have yet been considered where the issue of parallel, algorithm driven pricing has been considered, or where machine learning solutions have "independently" arrived at a cartelised price.

Undoubtedly regulators are live to the issues involved in the use of potentially autonomous agents in a competition context – the big question for the immediate and near-term future is the extent to which they will be able to identify anti-competitive behaviours and enforce them within existing competition law frameworks.

CHAPTER NINE
SECTOR SPECIFIC
CONSIDERATIONS

In this chapter we take a closer look at some additional legal considerations for Artificial Intelligence and machine learning in relation to particular sector-based applications.

Specifically we consider how machine learning is influencing the delivery of medicine and healthcare, as well as the disruption this technology is bringing to the retail, financial services, transportation and energy and infrastructure industries.

Lifesciences, Medicine and Healthcare

Artificial intelligence is bringing to life some particularly exciting applications in relation to the practice of medicine.

Broadly speaking, the AI applications in this sector can be divided into the following categories (and I have deliberately excluded drug discovery or pharmacological based innovation from this analysis): diagnostic classification or prediction through systematic review of patient related evidence such as medical imaging or symptomatic patient data, where the power of deep learning is harnessed to better identify the presence of or predict the incidence of disease; and IoT or "*internet of things*" chronic disease management systems, where AI powered applications monitor patient health and manage chronic conditions through automated drug delivery and regular information updates to healthcare professionals. It is in the first category that some of the most startling achievements have been made. "Deep Patient" for example, a program developed by researchers at Mount Sinai Hospital in New York, was provided with the records of 700,000 individuals as a training data set with a view to predicting disease in patients at the hospital. When presented with new records for examination, it proved to be very accurate – sometimes even predicting disease incidence for highly unpredictable conditions, such as schizophrenia that human medical professionals had difficulty in doing[184].

For now, the "*holy grail*" of direct surgical intervention (robotic surgery) where trained robots autonomously perform actual medical operations remains science fiction rather than fact, despite some interesting research which shows promise in the technology. The Da Vinci surgical robot, for example, which has been on the market for the last 15 years – actually depends upon remote actuation by human surgeon and "tunes out" autonomous movement on the basis that all procedures should be human directed.

Personal Data regulation – and in particular the GDPR features large in terms of the use of such applications, particularly when one considers that much of their utility is based on the treatment of individuals. Chapter three of this book (on Big Data and Artificial Intelligence) considers such regulation at length, however for the purposes of this chapter it is worth noting that a similar experiment to the one carried out at Mount Sinai hospital was attempted in the UK by the Royal Free NHS Foundation Trust – a collective of three major London hospitals. The Royal Free trust handed over 1.6 million patient records to Google's DeepMind project with a view to testing a system for detection and diagnosis of acute kidney injury. The UK's ICO ruled, when looking at the essential seven data protection principles, that this had been done in contravention of the Data Protection Act as, amongst other grounds, there was a lack of transparency in how the data used would be processed and insufficient measures had been taken to inform patients that their data would be used in clinical safety testing. In consequence, it was not reasonable to expect them to understand that their data would be used in this way. The ICO also found that the use of 1.6 million patient records was excessive and disproportionate. The Royal Free trust was ultimately asked to sign an undertaking in relation to its future use of patient data and to commission a third-party audit of the DeepMind trial.

In addition to data protection regulation, it is probably medical device

---

[184] Deep Patient: An Unsupervised Representation to Predict the Future of Patients from the Electronic Health Records, Miotto, Li, Kidd & Dudley, Scientific Reports 2016

regulation which impacts most upon the use of AI applications in this sector. EU regulation in this space is driven by a new Regulation on Medical Devices[185] and another on In Vitro Diagnostic Medical Devices[186]. The Medical Device Regulations, put in place a CE declaration of conformity scheme in respect of such devices which is in effect a mandatory quality assurance scheme to minimise risk and maximise safety in relation to their production, distribution, storage and use. The new Regulations introduce a harmonised EU approach, increase transparency by the introduction of an EU wide database of such devices to ensure transparency as well as bringing in new post and pre-market reporting and surveillance measures.

A "medical device" is defined by the current legislation as "*any instrument, apparatus, appliance, software, implant, reagent, material or other article intended by the manufacturer to be used, alone or in combination, for human beings for one or more of the following specific medical purposes:- diagnosis, prevention, monitoring, prediction, prognosis, treatment or alleviation of disease; diagnosis, monitoring, treatment, alleviation of, or compensation for, an injury or disability; investigation, replacement or modification of the anatomy or of a physiological or pathological process or state; providing information by means of in vitro examination of specimens derived from the human body, including organ, blood and tissue donations, and which does not achieve its principal intended action by pharmacological, immunological or metabolic means; in or on the human body, but which may be assisted in its function by such means...*"[187]. What is interesting from our viewpoint is that ECJ issued guidance in the *Snitem/Philips France* case[188] under the prior directives on Medical Devices[189] to the effect that standalone software not embodied in an apparatus should be treated as a medical device for the purposes of the legislation if "*the intended purpose, defined by the*

---

[185] Regulation EU 2017/745

[186] Regulation EU 2017/746

[187] Article 2 (1) of Regulation 2017/745

[188] C-329/16

[189] Directives 90/385/EEC on Active Implantable Medical Devices, Directive 93/42/EEC on Medical Devices and Directive 98/79/EC on In Vitro Diagnostic Medical Devices

manufacturer, is specifically medical"[190] – it is not enough if the software is general purpose but used in a medical setting (such as for example a word processing package used in a hospital).

Quite whether this provides sufficient clarity for use of artificially intelligent software-based systems when used in a medical context remains to be seen – particularly given the potentially general-purpose nature of some systems[191]. Paradoxically we could end up in a situation where the applicability of the legislation depends upon the context – so that a neural network trained on diagnostic patient data used in a hospital for the purpose of identifying disease is caught, whereas an ostensibly identical system trained on data which is designed to optimise the efficiency and regulate the environmental controls of the hospital building is not.

Pandemic Support

It would be remiss of course not to mention the significant role that AI and machine learning have played in what I would term *"pandemic support"* during the COVID-19 crisis.

This obviously intersects with the previous discussion on Lifesciences, Medicine and Healthcare, but is deserving of its own special mention as usage in support of pandemic management raises particular legal and ethical questions, many of which are wider than simply healthcare, such as the potential duality of use of the technology in such situations (for example potentially giving rise to the spectre of mass surveillance). These questions are particularly significant as in an emergency situation such as the COVID-19 crisis, it is easier to jump to hastily technologically led conclusions which would in ordinary times face potentially more public

---

[190] C-329/16 at paragraph 24

[191] See *When does stand-alone software qualify as a Medical Device in the European Union? – the CJEU's decision in Snitem and what it implies for the next generation of Medical Devices, Medical Law Review*, Volume 28, Issue 3, Summer 2020, Pages 615–624

scrutiny and scepticism[192].

The first such use is in the context of so called "*track and trace*" apps. These are apps that are designed to identify who has come into contact with an infected person and to warn them to self-isolate in the event of contact with an infected person. Although the primary technological basis for such apps is Bluetooth technology (which is used to determine proximity to other users), machine learning algorithms potentially have a role to play in providing more sophisticated personalised analysis of overall probability of exposure to the virus by reference to demographic, health data and user provided behavioural data.

Data acquisition from sources such as track and trace apps provides machine learning algorithms to undertake *Pandemic modeling*, itself a natural use case for these highly predictive technologies. Such models are incredibly useful not only from an epidemiological, statistical and research perspective to predict how the pandemic may impact a society at a wider level, they also provide scientists, politicians and others with decision authority the best way to achieve resource optimisation.

AI and machine learning tools have proved critical in improving health care responses by assisting in the evaluation and impact of disease progression in infected individuals and improving diagnoses (for example by using software to detect COVID-19 related lung problems in computer tomography scans).

Finally, and perhaps most critically, machine learning algorithms are speeding up the response to a cure to COVID-19, by allowing scientists to more quickly unpack the Coronavirus genome sequence and to provide for predictive AI research models to accelerate evaluation of promising vaccine candidates[193].

---

[192] These wider issues are considered at length in the Human Technology Foundation's report *Technology Governance in a time of Crisis: COVID-19 Related Decision Support*. See: https://www.itechlaw.org/sites/default/files/Final%20Report_ENGLISH.pdf

[193] See the Council of Europe publication on AI and control of Covid-19 coronavirus for a wider discussion https://www.coe.int/en/web/artificial-intelligence/ai-and-

Retail and Consumer

As we saw in Chapter eight (Market Distorting Effects – AI and Competition Law), much machine learning activity in the retail sector is driven by the price optimisation strategies which are being adopted by the major online retail platforms. Aside from these considerations, the sector is leading the way in machine learning powered CRM (or customer relationship management) – which could include the provision of chat bots or interactive intelligent customer platforms to assist in a pre- or post-sales environment or automated product recommendations. Artificial Intelligence is also optimising manufacturing, logistics and delivery and payment processes.

As with Medicine and Healthcare, much innovation in retail is also being driven by the increased sophistication with which machine learning applications can process personal data, so the topics debated in Chapter three (Big Data and Artificial Intelligence) are equally relevant here.

Aside from this, consumer and retail related regulation in the UK is focussed on consumer protection law (principally the Consumer Protection Act 1987) and consumer rights (the Consumer Rights Act 2015), both of which were discussed in detail in Chapter two (Causation and Artificial Intelligence) in the context of contractually based causation. The one area which is worth raising here are the new provisions in the Consumer Rights Act which may apply in a context where artificial intelligence solutions are being used in a retail context. Chapter 3 of that Act puts in place a range of provisions which relate to the supply of digital content and digital services[194]. Clearly these provisions are not intended merely to apply to machine learning solutions but in relation to anything which is supplied in a digital context.

Chapter 3 applies to *"a contract for a trader to supply digital content to a consumer, if it is supplied or to be supplied for a price paid by the consumer. (2) This Chapter also applies to a contract for a trader to supply digital content to a consumer, if (a) it is supplied free with goods or services or other*

control-of-covid-19-coronavirus

[194] Sections 33-47 of the Consumer Rights Act, 2015

digital content for which the consumer pays a price, and (b) it is not generally available to consumers unless they have paid a price for it or for goods or services or other digital content"[195].

A range of familiar statutory warranties and remedies are then provided, which align broadly to the warranties and remedies originating in the Sale of Goods Act 1893 and its successor statute, the Sale of Goods Act 1979, including warranties as to conformity with description, satisfactory quality and fitness for purpose (which we will return to in a moment), and remedies that provide for a right to a repair or a replacement[196], price reduction[197] or a refund[198]. Where dealing with consumers, these provisions cannot be contracted out of.[199]

So the scope of application would apply in relation to digital content paid for directly by a consumer – typically in the form of a digital download of software, or something which is "*bundled*" with either other digital content, services or a device. Clearly therefore, and to take a specific example by way of our immediate context, the provision of an Amazon Echo device with Amazon's voice service, Alexa would be caught.

Quite how useful these provisions actually are in the context of e.g. a digital voice assistant, remains to be seen. The law inevitably pre-dates the widespread availability of these AI powered services and pre-supposes an essentially static, predictable or linear performance in relation to the relevant digital content – so that for example a downloaded digital video should *play* without interruption or a piece of games software should *install and activate* on the hardware which it is downloaded to in accordance with its specification. An NLP (natural language processing) enabled AI

---

[195] Sections 33(1), 33(2) (a) & (b)

[196] Section 43, Consumer Rights Act 2015

[197] Section 44, Consumer Rights Act 2015

[198] Section 45, Consumer Rights Act 2015

[199] Section 47, Consumer Rights Act 2015

voice assistant will almost certainly be subject to a more complex assessment as to whether it is of *"satisfactory quality"*[200], *"fit for purpose"*[201] or *"in conformity with description"*[202]. Evidently one which does not function at all when the device within which it is installed is enabled fails these benchmarks. But what of one that lies, is inaccurate in its answers or utters profanities? These will be matters which will inevitably become the subject of future litigation.

It is apparent that the role of supplier statements, descriptions and disclaimers will become ever more critical in determining what is reasonable to expect when using such devices – Section 34(2) in the context of satisfactory quality provides that *"the quality of digital content is satisfactory if it meets the standard that a reasonable person would consider satisfactory, taking account of—*

(a) any description of the digital content, (b)the price mentioned in section 33(1) or (2)(b) (if relevant), and (c)all the other relevant circumstances (see subsection (5))." – Subsection (5) of the same section providing that *"the relevant circumstances mentioned in subsection (2)(c) include any public statement about the specific characteristics of the digital content made by the trader, the producer or any representative of the trader or the producer."*

Financial Services

The next sector which is worthy of some consideration is that of financial services. As we have seen in the context of some of the other discussions in this book, artificial intelligence is permeating and disrupting virtually every aspect of the financial services industry (see for example various discussions on the insurance industry in Chapters two, three and eight, above). Given the length of time that some level of automation has been available in the financial services industry, it is interesting to benchmark legislative responses in this sector against those sectors which are compar-

---

[200] Section 34, Consumer Rights Act 2015

[201] Section 35, Consumer Rights Act 2015

[202] Section 36, Consumer Rights Act 2015

atively less mature (or at least, where machine learning solutions are considered more novel).

For the purposes of this particular section, I intend however to focus briefly on two distinct aspects that are worthy of mention – one being algorithmic trading or "*robotrading*" and the other "*roboadvice*". As these names imply, these are either investment or advice-based services which are carried on fully autonomously or with some level of human intervention. It is important to note that not all of these services deploy sophisticated artificial intelligence or machine learning as part of their solution, but there is an increased tendency in the industry to do so.

Algorithmic trading exists because when used correctly, it provides significant advantages over traditional trading methods – specifically in relation to trading and execution speed and latency. These factors often make the difference between loss and profit in relation to financial trading, although there are concerns that without appropriate levels of oversight and supervision we could be led into other market falls such as the 2010 "*flash crash*" (generally accepted to have been caused by algorithmic traders), which caused a brief 36 minute crash in the Dow Jones and Nasdaq indices, momentarily causing them to lose around a trillion US dollars. The Markets in Financial Instruments Directive (or "MiFID"[203] as it is more commonly referred to in the industry), defines algorithmic trading as "*Trading in financial instruments which meets the following conditions: (a) where a computer algorithm automatically determines individual parameters of orders such as whether to initiate the order, the timing, price or quantity of the order or how to manage the order after its submission (b) there is limited or no human intervention does not include any system that is only used for the purpose of routing orders to one or more trading venues or the processing of orders involving no determination of any trading parameters or for the confirmation of orders or the post-trade processing of executed transactions.*"[204]. The legislative provisions of MiFID are sensibly pragmatic – reflecting the relative maturity of the use of such automated solutions in

---

[203] Technically MiFID is comprised of MiFID II, Directive 2014/65 EU, which came into force on January 3rd 2018, and MIFIR, the Markets in Financial Instruments Regulation 600/2014 EU

[204] Article 4(1) 39 of MiFID (2014/65/EU)

trading as opposed to some of the other legislative measures that we have discussed in other contexts. The MiFID requirements on algorithmic trading are embodied in UK law through the FCA's Market Conduct Sourcebook or "MAR" and the EU Commission Delegated Regulation 2017/589 which is referred to in the industry as "RTS 6". I do not propose to go into the details here but they are intended to introduce a governance and reporting framework for firms using such solutions and are designed to ensure safety (such as business continuity and *"kill switches"* where appropriate) as well as consistent systems and controls in order to prevent market abuse or disorderly markets.

Roboadvice or automated investment advice is the other area which has seen significant growth in recent years as the utility and flexibility of artificially intelligent powered solutions has increased. This is due to the fact that there is an increasing trend for consumers to take control of their own finances and to dispense with traditional intermediaries, such as financial advisors. In many cases, such consumers will be using online tools to determine whether or not they should invest in a particular product, and this puts the whole concept of automated advice and/or recommendations into the spotlight.

Typically the UK and European regulators makes no distinction for regulatory purposes between *investment advice* provided on a traditional basis, or via an automated solution. What has therefore been important for firms offering such *roboadvice* is determining in fact whether what they are offering is regulated investment advice and are caught by the regulatory regime, or *guidance,* which is essentially unregulated. This is often referred to as the *"advice boundary"*.

Since the publication of the last edition of this book, the FCA has taken on board the differences between the way in which this "advice boundary" is determined when taking into account Article 53 of the existing Financial Services and Markets Act 2000 (Regulated Activities) Order 2001 (the "Regulated Activities Order" or "RAO"), and MiFID. MiFID focusses on the provision of personal advice recommendations to an individual customer. The three main elements are that (i) there is a recommendation that is made to a person in their capacity as an investor or potential investor; (ii) it is based on the investor's personal circumstances and is presented as suitable when taking these personal circumstances into account; and (iii) the recommendation must relate to a type of investment which is a MiFID financial instrument[205]. The definition of advice under the prior version of the RAO in contrast however did not provide any requirement for advice to be of a personal nature.

Following the 2015 Financial Advice Market Review (the final evaluation report for which was published by the FCA in December 2020[206]) it was identified that there was a need to clarify the advice/guidance boundary. FAMR recommended that the definition within the RAO be aligned to the MiFID definition. The treasury subsequently undertook this amendment and amended the RAO, distinguishing regulated advice between advice that was based on personal recommendation and non-personalised advice. In addition to this, perimeter guidance was published by the FCA to help firms understand the boundary between these two forms of advice[207].

Transportation

In Chapter two, on Causation, we briefly covered on the UK government's legislative response to automation and transportation as embodied in the Autonomous and Electric Vehicles Act which attempts to clarify potential gaps in insurance cover liability when a vehicle is being piloted autonomously as opposed to a human driver[208]. Whilst this is a pragmatic response to an immediate problem caused by the use of such vehicles, it does not, as we explained at length in Chapter two, do much more than push causation issues directly into the laps of insurers who will still face

---

[205] See Section C, Annex I of MiFID (2014/65/EU) – generally transferrable securities, money market instruments, units in collective investment undertakings, options, futures, swaps, forward rate agreements and other derivative contracts.

[206] See *Evaluation of the impact of the Retail Distribution Review and the Financial Advice Market Review* https://www.fca.org.uk/publication/corporate/evaluation-of-the-impact-of-the-rdr-and-famr.pdf

[207] See FCA publication PS18/3, February 2018 – https://www.fca.org.uk/publication/policy/ps18-03.pdf

[208] Section 2 of the Autonomous and Electric Vehicles Act

considerable difficulties in pursuing claims against other third parties, including the manufacturers of such vehicles.

Chapter three, on Big Data, touched on the EU's *Strategy on Co-operative Intelligent Transport Systems* (*CIT-S*) which set out a policy vision in relation to smart vehicle communications infrastructure from a personal data management perspective. The EU Commission attempted in 2019 to introduce a Regulation to support Co-operative Intelligent Transport Systems[209], however that proposal was rejected by the European Council[210], partly it seems on the basis of lack of time for the legislative process to complete and partly due to the fact that the technology measures proposed by the Commission in the draft Regulation were perceived as limiting EU markets in intelligent transport systems to a particular technology. Quite what the Commission proposes as a replacement measure, if any, remains to be seen.

Aside from these two measures, the Law Commission of England and Wales in a joint project with the Law Commission for Scotland, have, at time of writing, been tasked by the Centre for Connected and Autonomous Vehicles (which is part of the Departments for Transport and Business, Energy and Industrial Strategy) to undertake a wide ranging review of the laws relating to the regulation and review of autonomous vehicles[211], in recognition of the inadequacies in the law discussed in the earlier chapters of this book.

The review will address concerns related to safety assurance mechanisms (such as type approvals and MoTs), accountability in terms of crime and accidents, and assessing how to decide whether such vehicles are safe for road use. Data protection and privacy issues, theft and cyber security and land use policy are expressly stated to be outside of the review's scope, as are drones and vehicles which are designed solely for use on pavements rather than roads. The review is currently in its third and final stage of

---

[209] 2019/2651 (DEA)

[210] See https://oeil.secure.europarl.europa.eu/oeil/popups/ficheprocedure.do?lang=en&reference=2019/2651(DEA)

[211] See https://www.lawcom.gov.uk/project/automated-vehicles/

consultation, which is currently scheduled to close on 18th March 2021. The final report is expected to be published in the last quarter of 2021.

Energy and Utilities

The energy sector has all the characteristics which would lend itself to effective implementation of machine learning technologies – the sector relies on a very large generation and distribution infrastructure – and also deals with significant amounts of personal data from consumers of those utilities. Automated trading in energy-based commodities is of course caught by the financial services considerations we discussed earlier in this chapter, and the use of artificially intelligent systems to price or recommend energy supplier "switches" for retail consumers may also touch the Competition considerations we looked at in the context of chapter eight, although it is worth bearing in mind that wholesale gas and electricity generation and distribution markets in the UK are monopolistic and that the regulator, Ofgem, has interposed itself into these by the imposition of price controls on transmission and distribution.

To date, there have been limited forays – smart home automation, both in terms of monitoring usage by way of *IoT* or *Internet of Things* enabled intelligent thermostatic devices and metering – so called "smart meters" are beginning to penetrate households and raise the same privacy and data protection implications for personal data management that we discussed in Chapter three.

"Smart grid" management of power distribution has the potential to revolutionise energy management from an environmental, cost and demand perspective, by for example increasing output when needed (or anticipating such spikes in demand) or shuttling capacity intelligently to where it is needed the most. Such smart grid technologies also have the benefit of potentially offering more sophisticated "real time" maintenance management (for example by reporting and predicting network points of failure) as well as providing enhanced monitoring to enable protection against what are perceived as an increased level of cyber security threats that threaten the integrity of utility networks. As of the date of writing, there are no specific legislative measures in contemplation within the UK to cover the use of such technologies in the Energy and Utilities sector,

which ultimately forces us back to reliance on current law and regulation.

Infrastructure and the Built Environment

The construction and property sectors are also undergoing a transformation with the steady implementation of artificial intelligence and machine learning solutions, part of the innovation wave collectively grouped under the "*Proptech*" banner.

As with the Energy and Utility sector, there is no consistent drive to regulate adoption of the technology, given the range of applications it could potentially influence, rather we must look to (or at least have an appreciation of) the impact of adoption in relation to specific areas, when mapped against existing laws and regulations.

There are four growing areas in the construction and property sectors where machine learning tools are beginning to make their mark. The first is in relation to automated building information modelling which is typically applied during the construction of a building, the second is in relation to automated property portfolio valuation for investors, the third applies to so-called *Smart Cities*, and the fourth is in relation to facilities management.

Building Information Modelling

Building information modelling (or BIM) tools put simply allow the automation of complex design and modelling when preparing architectural plans for a new building. Such tools enable construction professionals to more accurately and efficiently make use of materials (through for example automated computation of loading stresses); refine construction processes to optimise routing of utilities (such as power and water) and enhance green or environmental profiles (through for example maximal space efficiency and configuration). Machine learning tools enhance BIM by the introduction of predictive and classification capabilities – identifying where components and/or materials selected are incorrect or missing or predicting (by reference to the immediate context of the proposed building) where prior conditions have been deemed to be unsafe.

From a regulatory and legal compliance perspective BIM tools clearly have the potential to enhance safety when constructing buildings but equally speaking blind reliance on such tools will not absolve the user from liability should they fail. As noted elsewhere in this book and in other contexts, it is for the user to re-assure themselves that the tool has the appropriate level of accreditation and certification and to bear in mind that all of the previous issues we have discussed in relation to the inherent "black box" nature of machine learning solutions also applies equally here.

Automated Property Portfolio Valuation

Automated Property Portfolio Valuation (or APPV) uses algorithms to analyze the façade of building, and draws on multiple data sources to estimate the building's age, size and quality, as well as its location to predict rental yield or market value, with high degrees of accuracy, utilising techniques which are similar to human-based visual processing[212].

Smart Cities

The term Smart City refers to the smart or intelligent management of municipal infrastructure through the use of technologies such as artificial intelligence and IoT or internet of things. Smart Cities optimise connectivity (so called *hyperconnectivity*) between city infrastructure and buildings, as well as autonomous vehicles and the city's human visitors and residents. I mention this for completeness here only as the implications of such smart infrastructure are far more wide-ranging than artificial intelligence – however that technology has a key part to play in optimising the operational management of such municipalities[213].

---

[212] *OfficeBlocks*, a commercial implementation of APPV, was launched in Singapore in October 2020 as part of a joint collaboration between property consultancy JLL and Risk Integrated.

[213] Saudi Arabia has recently announced a visionary smart city program called "*The Line*". This is intended to be a 106-mile belt of communities, connected without the need for cars or roads. As described by the Crown Prince of Saudi Arabia, Mohammed bin Salman, The Line will be completely free of cars and streets, with residents given access to nature and all of their daily needs within a walking distance of five minutes. This '*linear development of hyper-connected AI-enabled communities*' is

Facilities Management

The final area in the property sector which is being influenced by artificial intelligence is in the provision of facilities management or FM solutions. Clearly the provision of services to any large building is highly labour intensive and therefore ripe for automation. Some examples of this might include *security systems* – using AI to monitor facilities and permit access to buildings; *cleaning and maintenance* – deploying automated solutions (including drones or robots) to clean internal and external surfaces and to spot and/or predict where maintenance to the building is needed; *reception services* – dealing with visitors to the building and handing off to appropriate hosts; and *logistics and waste management* – managing deliveries to the building and removing refuse. The other area where machine learning solutions can benefit use of buildings is by the optimisation of space (through the identification of underutilisation or overutilisation) in particular in a business environment where hot desking is the norm. All of these solutions now exist in a commercial form to a greater or lesser degree. For a wider discussion on automated service provision , which will be relevant to this section, please see Chapter ten.

---

intended to be powered by 100% clean energy.

CHAPTER TEN
AUTOMATION AND AI
SERVICE PROVISION

In this chapter we focus on the evolution of third-party AI service provision. The machine learning and AI market is increasingly moving in this direction: away from bespoke systems created by businesses and towards commoditised 'off the shelf' machine learning based service offers – in much the same way as the ERP (enterprise resource planning) and CRM (customer relationship management) markets have evolved over the last twenty or so years[214].

Robotic Process Outsourcing

Robotic process outsourcing, or robotic process automation ("**RPO**") is not a new concept – it refers to the deployment of automation, whether that be robots or other machines, to replace humans in task-based processes. Typically, RPOs have a hybrid characteristic in that they tend to deliver managed services through a combination of human workers with an automated element.

Industries such as manufacturing have been using progressively complex degrees of automation since the time of the industrial revolution in the early 19th century. Robotic assembly of motor vehicles was pioneered in the mid to late 1960s with the use of spotwelding robots by General Motors, quickly followed by more flexible and microprocessor-controlled units in the mid-1970s. By the mid-1980s the industry had been transformed.

What machine learning brings to robotic process outsourcing is the ability for robots to assume significantly more complex tasks to those that have previously been undertaken. To continue the car manufacturing

---

214 Whereas once this was the domain of bespoke developers, these markets are now dominated by global companies SAP and Oracle.

analogy, many such robots are now semi-autonomous, with degrees of environment processing, enabling flexible interaction with a changing environment that are at least equivalent to the autonomous vehicles currently being launched on the driving market.

We should not however confine our perspective to manufacturing. Machine learning is opening markets to RPO that have hitherto only been able to be automated on a limited basis, such as the provision of semi-professional tasks involving a high degree of human interaction – front office skills such as call centre and helpdesk operatives for example. The prediction is that ultimately professional level skills will be open to automation, such as those currently practiced by lawyers and accountants.

There are real and complex political and moral arguments at play with ever increasing waves of automation replacing human workers, and the workplace is under a degree of existential threat in the mid to near future the likes of which have not been seen since the industrial revolution. This is a book however about the practical legal consequences of the deployment of such technology. In this sense, outside the other issues that we have analysed in this book, these disruptive considerations are no more different (or at least equivalent to) the considerations that have to be managed when outsourcing in the traditional sense.

Conventional outsourcing, for the uninitiated, entails the transfer of an internally managed service or operation to an external service provider. When introducing automation and artificial intelligence into the workplace, what therefore are the primary practical legal consequences that need to be borne in mind? The first and by far away the most significant consideration is the management of workforce displacement.

Typically in a conventional outsourcing carried out within the UK (and indeed the wider EU), when a service is outsourced, the rights embodied in the EU's Transfers of Undertakings Directive[215] and enacted in the UK under the Transfer of Undertakings (Protection of Employment) Regulations 2006[216]. Broadly speaking, this stipulates that (unlike many

---

[215] 2001/23/EC

[216] SI 2006/246

jurisdictions where employment is "*at will*", such as the United States), when an "*undertaking*"[217] is transferred from customer to service provider (a "*relevant transfer*"), the employment of those employees carrying out the service immediately prior to the transfer is carried over to the service provider, without any break in continuity, thus preserving their extant employment rights. This means that the service provider must continue their employment on equivalent terms. Any dismissals carried out because of a relevant transfer are deemed to be unfair unless there is an *economic, technical* or *organisational* reason for the dismissals which for the purposes of the legislation[218] are deemed to justified. In such circumstances, the affected employee is considered to be redundant and may be entitled to statutory compensation if they have been employed for a continuous period of more than two years[219].

Plainly in the case of robotic displacement, there is no transfer of undertaking, no continuity of employment and redundancy or redeployment of the affected employees is the only option available to the employer. The Employment Rights Act provides as follows: "*For the purposes of this Act an employee who is dismissed shall be taken to be dismissed by reason of redundancy if the dismissal is wholly or mainly attributable to— (a) the fact that his employer has ceased or intends to cease—(i) to carry on the business for the purposes of which the employee was employed by him, or (ii) to carry on that business in the place where the employee was so employed, or (b) the fact that the requirements of that business—(i) for employees to carry out work of a particular kind, or (ii) for employees to carry out work of a particular kind in the place where the employee was employed by the employer, have ceased or diminished or are expected to cease or diminish.*"[220]. The Act continues with the following embellishment: "*In subsection (1) "cease" and "diminish" mean cease and diminish either permanently or temporarily and*

---

[217] There is much UK and EU law on what constitutes an undertaking, but essentially this is the business operation engaged in economic activities which is to be transferred to the service provider, see further *Höfner & Elser v. Macrotron GmbH [1991] ECR I-1979*

[218] See the Employment Rights Act 1996, s98(2)(c)

[219] s135 Employment Rights Act 1996

[220] s139(1) Employment Rights Act 1996

for whatever reason."[221].

Somewhat perversely this does mean that in terms of justifying grounds for redundancy, the law makes it demonstrably easier to do so in circumstances where a machine is to replace a person.

Whether this will ultimately lead to a public policy change in the event of widespread displacement remains to be seen – already there has been some debate in the UK and the USA about the introduction of a "*workplace automation*" tax, to help fund the retraining of displaced employees. South Korea has taken the first tentative steps on this path by implementing an indirect tax on workplace automation by applying in effect a reduced tax incentive benefit to workplaces originally designed to boost productivity[222]. Somewhat more radically, some economists have suggested going further and have advocated the introduction of a universal basic income as a solution to the inequality and inevitable work displacement caused by the emergence of robots and artificial intelligence[223].

Outside of workplace displacement, what are the other problematic issues which will need to be resolved when outsourcing to artificial intelligence?

Many of these will revolve around the nature of the task and duties which have been delegated. As has been apparent throughout previous chapters of this book – there are going to be specific duties and responsibilities which cannot yet be transferred to a machine learning system because the law has not yet developed a coherent theory of artificial *personhood*. This is likely to be a hugely important step if we are to confer onto machines the responsibility to make decisions which have real (ie. legal and moral) consequences for human beings. Unless and until the law evolves in this

---

[221] s139(6) Employment Rights Act 1996

[222] See http://www.koreatimes.co.kr/www/news/tech/2017/08/133_234312.html
"*Korea takes first step to introduce 'Robot Tax'*"

[223] The suggestion was made by professor Sir Christopher Pissarides, a Nobel laureate and the Regius professor at the London School of Economics during the World Economic Forum in Davos, 20th January 2016

way (and it is looking increasingly like a more distant prospect[224]), ultimately what can be outsourced will necessarily be constrained, and we will be left with activities and tasks that are not (or are at least, minimally) regulated.

Aside from these considerations, outsourcing agreements contain a variety of supplier focussed contractual obligations and liabilities to be managed which in theory could be extended to artificially intelligent systems – although some thought would need to be given to their application. Many of the areas which are likely to be applicable have already been discussed at length elsewhere in this book. These include the compliance issues around big data analytics (see the commentary in Chapter three) and the protection and management of intellectual property, both in relation to deliverables created by the machine learning system in the course of the provision of the outsourced services (which as we discussed previously would likely be covered, certainly in the UK by the machine generated copyright provisions of the Copyright, Designs and Patents Act 1988[225]) and in respect of the machine learning system itself (again, see the commentary in Chapter five). Consideration would also need to be given to ongoing service management and Service Level agreements (or SLAs) as these are a feature of most traditional outsourcing agreements. As the name implies, these enforce mandated levels of service performance upon suppliers to ensure that the services being performed do not drop below a particular standard. Whereas in traditional outsourcing agreements these typically are focussed on *direct performance by the supplier of the services*, there is an increasing trend in complex RPOs for these to translate to *maintenance and support of the AI system performing the service*, as these are typically the non-AI (human based) services which are performed in an RPO context and which can be enforced in a traditional manner. Interestingly, in terms of SLA and contract enforcement in RPO there is a potential role to play here for another upcoming technology, so called block-chain enabled *"smart contract"* systems. Initiatives such as the Accord Project[226] an international working party made up of several

---

[224] See the debate in Chapter two on artificial personhood

[225] See s178 of the CDPA 1988 and s9(3) respectively

[226] See https://www.accordproject.org/

law firms and technology businesses are looking to develop open-source technology standards to transition contracts from static documents into fully integrated components of commercial systems – which would mean for example – automatic deduction or "netting off" of service credits in the event that a particular service level was not met, without human intervention.

Artificial Intelligence as a Service (AIaaS)

One of the biggest blocks to date to small and medium sized enterprise in the deployment of machine learning systems and tools has been the level of investment and expertise that is required to successfully build and train such systems. Unsurprisingly this requires a degree of specialist skill that is beyond the means of most in the SME sector and possibly even some larger businesses – it is also in many cases, *"non-core"* in terms of business objectives.

Coupled with this has been a strong trend in the outsourcing market, driven by ubiquity in cloud computing, to move away from traditional *"on premise"* solutions to service based *"on demand"* SaaS (Software as a Service) solutions or Cloud based architecture for the delivery of complex managed services.

As machine learning systems become ever more complex and capable we are seeing in turn a complex re-imagining and commoditisation of service delivery related tools and products and the emergence of artificial intelligence as a service or "AIaaS". What AIaaS attempts to offer is a commoditised cognitive computing platform, delivered via the cloud, that allows businesses to leverage the power of pre-built and trained machine learning solutions, either directly, or as part of a robotic process outsourcing via a third party.

AIaaS solutions are broadly speaking structured either as data, compute or pre-packaged services. AIaaS data solutions provide the convenience of ready-made pools of data to enable fast and effective training of machine learning models for common or generic problems – these might for example be comprised of masses of facial images for facial recognition applications. Compute services enable common infrastructural computing tasks to be carried out that are closely integrated with machine learning solutions – such as batch processing. Pre-packaged AIaaS allows for the provision of ready-made AI applications on demand that can be integrated into enterprise offerings.

Use of AIaaS solutions, whether pre-packaged or via data or compute models clearly brings convenience and speed of implementation to many "standard" machine learning solutions, such as facial recognition, language translation or natural language processing. However from a legal perspective such solutions introduce additional levels of difficulty to what may already be a significantly complex RPO arrangement. Numerous issues spring to mind – as a licensee of AIaaS data services you will need to be able to seek sufficient reassurance that the pools of training data that may be provided by the platform provider are sufficiently curated to avoid bias but have not been overfitted. Equally speaking, if you are seeking to include a commoditised application to support a facial recognition application, you will need to have specific assurance that the application has been adequately trained. Disclosure levels and transparency are likely to be key determinants for the customers of AIaaS providers, but equally speaking will prove to be a very difficult interface for the platform providers themselves to navigate, who will be naturally incentivised to keep as much confidential as possible, for fear of giving away valuable proprietary information.

Complex decision-making machine learning systems are likely to be harder to manage from a liability perspective if they are dependent upon AIaaS offerings, whether or not they form part of an RPO. Generally speaking, that is because in the event of a contract default – or even circumstances where you need to be able to justify or explain the consequences of a particular decision to an external third party, such as a regulator, you will be faced with having to work back through the licence terms granting access to the AIaaS platform. You will then have to determine the extent to which the provider of the AIaaS cognitive computing platform itself (with all the inherent difficulties we have already discussed in terms of "*black boxes*" and causation) is willing or able to provide an explanation or demonstrate that it is not the cause of the relevant default

– not of itself a trivial problem[227].

As I noted above, AIaaS platforms that are used in this way tend to be heavily proprietary and confidential, and the services they offer are often provided on a *"take it or leave it basis"*. As such it seems unlikely that you will be able to open the lid of the black box and peer inside should something unexpected occur. In fact the licences granted in such circumstances are typically drafted defensively to protect the platform provider.

I would add as a final caveat that we are in the early stages of the evolution of such services. It seems likely that such large platform providers may have to provide a *de minimis* level of transparency in order to establish credibility in their service offers and also to justify their compliance with law and use in regulated contexts.

MLOps

Whereas AIaaS describes the delivery of artificial intelligence by a third party to an enterprise customer, MLOps can be distinguished as the practice of embedding commoditised enterprise AI within such customers.

MLOps is a relatively new discipline and is based on the existing DevOps process of integrating IT (that is to say the process of deploying, running, and sometimes writing, applications) within an enterprise[228].

Many businesses now have the capability to leverage "self-serve" AI tools, such as pre-configured models and datasets from open source hosts such as Github and the Linux Foundation in order to create tailored AI tools.

MLOps in essence is a production lifecycle focussed on the granular activities and methodology involved in a successful machine learning integration.

Businesses that adopt MLOps can rapidly, frequently and reliably build

---

[227] Recall the refusal of Equivant, developers of COMPAS, a parole evaluation system, to release details of its internal operations. See Chapter seven.

[228] See *What is MLOps?* https://blogs.nvidia.com/blog/2020/09/03/what-is-mlops/

test and release machine learning into production on an operationalised basis. This might include standardising activities such as data collection, data ingestion, analysis and curation; and validating data and labelling data, as well as model training and model evaluation, eventually leading to full machine learning system deployment[229]. Seldon Core is an example of an open-source enterprise platform which makes use of MLOps for rapid deployment of machine learning models[230]. It utilises Kubernetes (essentially an open-source containerised orchestration system)[231] for automated application deployment.

Any analysis of MLOps from a legal risk perspective is likely to be highly dependent on the circumstances of a particular deployment. As the process is closely aligned to (if not exclusively) the use of open-source models and data, standard intellectual property open-source considerations will apply in relation to the extent to which subsequent use and exploitation of AI tools developed in this way may be restricted (for example there is likely to be a difference in treatment between AI tools developed for 'in house' use as opposed to those which are intended to be sold on as commercial products). As such a detailed understanding of the underlying open-source licence type is likely to be essential.

---

[229] Ibid., note 12

[230] See www.seldon.io

[231] Kubernetes or K8s was named after the Greek word for the helmsman of a ship or pilot and was developed by Google Native Cloud Foundation

CHAPTER ELEVEN
ARTIFICIAL INTELLIGENCE
AND CORPORATE LAW

In this chapter on Corporate law we take a closer look at the extent to which machine learning solutions are taking over human duties, both inside and outside the boardroom, whether by direct appointment as directors, or as delegates of the duties owed by directors to their companies and shareholders.

The cybernetic corporation

Before we look more closely at directors and their duties however, it is worth sketching a picture of the holy grail of automation in a corporate context (or nightmare depending upon your point of view). This is of course the fully cybernetic corporation. A cybernetic corporation is essentially a corporate machine – where all of the duties of the directors and employees are subsumed and taken over by artificial intelligence and robots undertake all necessary interaction with the physical world – such as fulfilment, logistics and call centre management. Decentralised Autonomous Organisations or DAOs take the concept one stage further and apply blockchain verification technologies to the decisions of such corporatized machines[232].

Clearly this is the stuff of science fiction and we are not yet at a stage where these entities can sustainably exist (other than in terms of early experimentation) – however there are signs that machine learning is beginning to encroach into corporate governance.

---

[232] The original DAO was an investor directed venture capital fund which launched in April 2016 and became defunct in September 2016. The code of the DAO was open-source. It had no conventional management structure or board of directors, was instantiated on the Ethereum blockchain and was effectively stateless. See *Experiments in Algorithmic Governance: A History and ethnography of 'the DAO' a failed Decentralized Autonomous Organisation*, Quinn DuPont, Univ. Toronto

Appointment of artificial intelligence systems as company directors

There are already reports of artificial intelligence systems being "appointed" to boards, either as directors or as observers. In 2016 for example the Nordic financial services company Tieto Corporation appointed the AI *Alicia T*, as "*a member of its leadership team*" and became the first company in Europe to do so. Tieto however was preceded by Deep Knowledge Ventures in Hong Kong who had in 2014 appointed an AI named *Vital* (Validating Investment Tool for Advancing Life Sciences) as an "*observer*" over their board of directors.

What then is the current status of artificial intelligence in the boardroom? Could machine learning systems be conceivably appointed as directors?

So far as the law of England and Wales is concerned this question is governed by the Companies Act 2006 rather inconclusively, which provides that "*(1) a private company must have at least one director. (2) a public company must have at least two directors.*"[233] and "*(1) a company must have at least one director who is a natural person. (2) this requirement is met if the office of director is held by a natural person as a corporation sole or otherwise by virtue of an office*"[234].

Whilst not explicitly provided for it is evident from its subsequent provisions that the Companies Act only contemplates the appointment of natural and legal persons (ie bodies corporate) as directors. This is because sections 163 and 164 respectively only describe the particulars of natural and legal persons that need to be entered into the company's register of directors.

It appears that so far as AI is concerned, machine learning systems will not (at least in the UK) be entitled to be directly appointed as directors. This is because, as we have previously considered in other contexts, no theory of *artificial personhood* equivalent to legal personality for corporations has yet been developed to confer upon them legal status (for more on this, please see Chapter two under the heading entitled "*Individuation*

---

[233] Section 154 of the Companies Act 2006

[234] Section 155 of the Companies Act 2006

or Artificial Personhood").

The next question to consider in terms of immediate impact in the board-room is the extent to which the use of machine learning in a corporate governance context is permitted when one takes into account the fiduci-ary and statutory duties which are owed by directors to the boards of the companies they are appointed to.

Delegation

Before we discuss the duties themselves, it is probably worth looking briefly at the extent to which directors can delegate those duties – as this will be of immediate relevance to our discussion. Table A (the model form of articles of association prescribed under UK companies legisla-tion[235]) allows directors the ability to delegate their duties as follows: " *(1) Subject to the articles, the directors may delegate any of the powers which are conferred on them under the articles— (a) to such person or committee; (b) by such means (including by power of attorney); (c) to such an extent; (d) in relation to such matters or territories; and (e) on such terms and conditions; as they think fit. (2) If the directors so specify, any such delegation may au-thorise further delegation of the directors' powers by any person to whom they are delegated. (3) The directors may revoke any delegation in whole or part, or alter its terms and conditions*"[236]. It seems apparent then that so far as delegation is concerned, the law simply does not contemplate these duties being taken over by anything other than a legal or natural person or com-mittee. We are effectively in the same position we discussed earlier in the context of the direct appointment of AIs as directors. Unless there is an evolution to grant some form of artificial personhood to machine learn-ing solutions, this will not be possible. This does not prevent of course artificial intelligence being used in the context of corporate governance – merely that if it is used, the legal basis will have little more significance than if a director used an ordinary computer in the context of his or her duties – AI in essence in this sense becomes transparent and is relegated to a tool or instrumental extension to be utilised. The individual director

---

[235] See the Companies (Model Articles) Regulations 2008

[236] See article 5 of the Model Articles for companies limited by shares

remains, in these circumstances, fully accountable and responsible for his or her acts.

Director's general duties

So far as the duties themselves are concerned, the Companies Act sets out several key "general" duties – as previously stated in different contexts, I don't propose to list them all here, but rather to concentrate on the ones which may be potentially significant in relation to the use of machine learning. These are the three general duties which are relevant – to *promote the success of the company* (to behave in a way most likely to promote the success of the company)[237]; to *exercise independent judgment*[238]; and to *exercise reasonable care, skill and diligence*[239].

Evidently there is already sufficient anecdotal evidence in the market to suggest that the effective deployment of machine learning solutions in the enterprise can have very beneficial effects in terms of optimising performance and efficiency.

As use of machine learning becomes more and more widespread and such systems become more and more capable it seems likely that the need for directors to advocate the use of such tools within their corporations in order to *promote the success of the company* is likely to grow and that this duty will become commensurately stronger. What is interesting however is that in large part much of the usefulness of machine learning solutions lies in their ability to predict or to provide real-time analysis in relation to a particular situation – in short a *judgmental view*, and potentially the ability to do this more accurately than any human being. It would seem therefore that this has the very real potential to conflict with the other duty I have called out above, the need to *exercise independent judgment*. This duty was originally created to prevent bias or narrow partisanship on the part of a director and his or her decisions – being beholden to one stakeholder or interest or their appointing shareholder at the expense of

---

[237] Section 172 Companies Act 2006

[238] Section 173 Companies Act 2006

[239] Section 174 Companies Act 2006

all others was unlikely to further the overarching interests of the company in a good sense – but equally speaking one can see how blind adherence to the decisions of a machine learning system, without necessarily exercising a critical review or promoting an alternative approach could also cause a director to fall into the same trap.

There is of course, a similar tautology in relation to the last of the director's duties that we discuss in this chapter – that of *exercising reasonable skill, care and diligence*. Again one can see how the duty might promote increased use of artificial intelligence in the boardroom if it leads to more efficient, rounded and evaluated decisions – in effect enhancing skill and diligence. Misapplied however, it might lead to a completely contrary result and ultimately breach of that duty. As in previous discussions in this book, context, use and application are critical to the successful deployment and utilisation of AI.

Transactional considerations – automated due diligence

Corporate transactions are of course an important feature of this legal landscape – companies and ownership are not static and invariably they will be subject to mergers, acquisitions, divestments and re-organisations. Machine learning has a role to play in this environment as well – principally around one of the key activities involved in any such deal – the corporate due diligence exercise. Typically this involves a detailed analysis and investigation of all of the debts, liabilities and assets of the corporate entity that is either being sold, purchased or merged – usually the exercise is split into three different parts – *financial* which focusses on verifying the financial information provided by the counterparty and to assess the underlying performance of the business; *commercial* which considers the market in which the target business sits and the potential competitive landscape; and *legal* which considers all of the legal elements of the transaction. This might cover for example the contracts that the business holds from customers; employment contracts with key employees; real property documentation such as leases; critical supply agreements into the business; how any intellectual property assets might be held and any actual or pending litigation.

Machine learning solutions are becoming more ubiquitous in relation to financial and legal due diligence exercises, leading many journalists of hyperbolic predisposition to prematurely predict the end of either lawyers or accountants or both. What these solutions do is ingest and filter the relevant financial or legal information on an automated basis into a pre-structured due diligence report. Typically this avoids the need for armies of junior lawyers or accountants to review the information manually to produce the same digest[240].

Generally speaking, automating the due diligence process also allows for significant increases in speed (machine learning solutions tend to be quicker than human beings) and decreases in cost (machine learning solutions are not paid by the hour as are legal or financial professionals but are subject to a licensing fee which tends to be much lower). There are therefore significant and apparent business benefits to introducing these processes into corporate transactions – I would however strike a note of caution and ask you the reader to cast your mind back to the contents of Chapter one. All machine learning based artificial intelligence requires significant and competent training in order to achieve good results. If the automated due diligence system that is deployed in a particular transaction has not been trained properly then the result it produces will at best be poor and at worst plain wrong. Given the professional duties that are owed by both accountancy firms and law firms to their clients – and in particular to act in the client's best interests, and also the potential for clients to initiate professional misconduct proceedings, it would seem sensible as a basic minimum to ensure that proper steps have been taken to verify that any machine learning system which is used has been properly tested and trained. In many cases it may actually be sensible for the professional advisor to go one step further and double check the actual automated due diligence report produced (which may perversely completely undermine the business rationales of speed and cost discussed earlier). I would suggest that the worst course of conduct is to accept any such report *"in blind faith"*.

---

[240] Market leading solutions include the diligence platforms provided by Luminance – see www.luminance.com and Kira – see www.kirasystems.com

CHAPTER TWELVE
POLITICAL, REGULATORY AND
INDUSTRY RESPONSES

As I mentioned right back in Chapter one, and to some degree predicted in the last edition of this book, the degree and extent of regulation (or at least proposed regulation) of artificial intelligence and machine learning technologies has moved significantly – indeed to such an extent that it now deserves a chapter in its own right.

Please bear in mind that much of this discussion is ongoing within the relevant organisations and or governmental regulators, so will be subject to change and adaptation. This discussion is also limited to those initiatives which are deemed to be of sufficient significance to merit a mention – it is not by any means a complete and exhaustive exposition.

I would hope however that many initiatives are sufficiently matured to enable a perspective on where the ultimate regulatory destination will be. With that in mind, there are a number of initiatives that are worth mentioning, as they reflect well some of the issues and concerns raised in this book.

Industry Initiatives

The Partnership on AI

The first, and possibly the most significant is the Partnership on AI or "PAI"[241] which has been established between Google, Microsoft, Apple, Amazon, IBM and Facebook (together with a number of other leading industry participants). The PAI attempts broadly to ensure that industry leaders in the development of AI do so on an ethical basis, taking into account a number of thematic "pillars" or priorities. These pillars include establishing conventions for safety in the use of AI and robotic systems

---

[241] See www.partnershiponai.org

(a key element of which is ensuring that AI systems cede gracefully when they fail rather than putting the user in a catastrophic position); making AI fair, transparent and accountable (in order to increase the auditability of decisions taken by AI systems); promoting co-operative AI systems; examining the way in which AI will influence the distribution of jobs and the nature of work – with a view to minimising disruption; investigating augmented systems that work collaboratively between humans and AI and variously considering the extent to which AI will influence society to ensure that it is for the greater good[242]. Members of the Partnership on AI also commit to uphold a set of eight tenets which attempt to define the way in which they approach the development and use of the technology[243]. These tenets aspirationally set admirable goals, however it remains to be seen how the members will apply these in practice.

OpenAI

OpenAI[244] is a non-profit AI research company which is focussed on developing AGI or artificial general intelligence. OpenAI, which was founded in 2015 jointly by entrepreneurs Sam Altman and Elon Musk, has been set up to counteract the concentrative effect of big corporation research into AI technologies and to ensure that AGI will ultimately benefit all of humanity. As I mentioned in the last edition of this book, OpenAI is governed by a Charter of principles which reflect this cautious approach to the development of AGI[245]. The Charter focusses on four

---

[242] See https://partnershiponai.org/about/

[243] The tenets are extracted at https://partnershiponai.org/tenets/ and can be summarised as follows 1) seeking to ensure that AI benefits and empowers as many people as possible 2) educating and listening to the public and engaging stakeholders 3) committing to open research and dialogue on ethical, social, economic and legal implications of AI 4) making R&D accountable 5) ensuring that domain specific concerns are addressed 6) addressing the challenges of AI by working to protect privacy; understanding all interests; making R&D socially responsible; making sure the technology is robust, reliable & trustworthy; and opposing use and development which would violate human rights 7) making AI understandable and interpretable and 8) striving to create a culture of co-operation trust and openness amongst AI scientists

[244] https://openai.com

[245] See https://openai.com/charter/

core principles – "*Broadly distributed benefits*" (ensuring that AGI is used for the benefit of all, avoiding uses which will harm humanity) "*Long-Term Safety*" (avoiding the development of AGI becoming a competitive race without time for adequate safety precautions) "*Technical Leadership*" (ensuring that OpenAI remains at the cutting edge of technology developments) and "*Co-operative Orientation*" (promoting active co-operation with other research and policy institutions).

Political and Regulatory Initiatives

The EU

Since the publication of the first edition of this book, the European Union has driven its legislative strategy for artificial intelligence significantly forward. Ursula Von Der Leyen assumed the EU Commission presidency on 1st December 2019, with a bold statement that within 100 days of taking over that "*a co-ordinated European approach on the human and ethical implications of Artificial Intelligence*"[246] would be developed.

This culminated recently in the publication of a much-vaunted white paper on Artificial Intelligence in February 2020[247]. The White Paper (as we shall refer to it) has the potential to significantly transform the way in which AI systems are regulated within the EU. As we shall see from the following discussion, it is designed largely to work in symbiosis with the EU's General Data Protection Regulation, or GDPR[248], which provides a similar overarching framework for personally identifiable information.

It does appear however that the Commission's grand strategy has been temporarily halted due to internal concerns expressed by some of the EU

---

[246] See https://ec.europa.eu/info/sites/info/files/president-elect-speech_de.pdf for text of the original speech (in German)

[247] White Paper on Artificial Intelligence – A European approach to excellence and trust COM (2020) 65 final, 19.2.2020 available at https://ec.europa.eu/info/sites/info/files/commission-white-paper-artificial-intelligence-feb2020_en.pdf

[248] Regulation (EU) 2016/679

member states. In a so-called "non paper" entitled "*Innovative and Trustworthy AI: Two Sides of the Same Coin*", sent to the Commission in early August 2020, 13 member states[249] argue strongly for a "soft law" approach to AI regulation, adopting existing laws as far as is practicable.

The key concern of these member states is that the strong unitary approach advocated by the Commission (as we discuss further below) could potentially act to stifle innovation in AI industries within Europe.

Notwithstanding this hiatus in regulatory approach, it is worth discussing the EU's White Paper in a little more detail to see where the potential legislative landscape could lie.

The White Paper attempts to put in place both an EU- wide strategy for investment in the new technologies as well as a policy structure to address the risks caused by its use. These two elements are referred to respectively as an "*ecosystem of excellence*" and an "*ecosystem of trust*".[250]

Given the success of the GDPR in extra territorial terms, it seems likely that any legislation coming out of the EU as part of the White Paper will have a similar impact and shape global regulatory responses to artificial intelligence. In fact, this would appear to be the overt intent of the EU in promoting it[251].

Whilst the "*ecosystem of excellence*" focusses on a variety of investment and skills led measures to attempt to "level up" the EU in the face of perceived disadvantages as against the US and China, such as the creation of so-called digital innovation hubs, and partnerships with academia as well as the public and private sectors[252], it is the proposed risk framework or

---

[249] Denmark, Belgium, the Czech Republic, Finland, France, Estonia, Ireland, Latvia, Luxembourg, the Netherlands, Poland, Portugal, Spain and Sweden.

[250] EU White Paper, page 3

[251] See Ursula Von Der Leyen's inaugural speech (note 8, supra) "*With the General Data Protection Regulation we set the pattern for the world. We have to do the same with artificial intelligence.*"

[252] EU White Paper, page 5 et seq

"ecosystem of trust" which is of most interest in this context.

The suggested rules-based framework draws heavily on two prior publications. The first was issued by the Commission's High Level Expert Group (or "HLEG") and is a set of guidelines on trustworthy AI, released in April 2019[253]. The second is a report from the Commission on the safety and liability implications of Artificial Intelligence, the internet of things and robotics, published at the same time as the White Paper[254].

From a review of the publication it is clear that the EU is advocating a risk-based approach to AI regulation – as the White Paper itself states *"As a matter of principle, the new regulatory framework for AI should be effective to achieve its objectives while not being excessively prescriptive so that it could create a disproportionate burden…"*[255]

This risk-based approach is essentially categorised by the Commission into two cumulative limbs. Firstly, appropriate regulation needs to be directed to those sectors where the use of AI could typically give rise to significant risks from the viewpoint of safety, consumer rights and fundamental rights (such as for example autonomous transportation, or healthcare). Secondly regulation should be applied where the actual use case proposed is likely *itself* to give rise to significant risk – which reflects the fact that not every use in every "high risk" sector will of course generate significant risk.

Of course, the Commission makes the additional reverse point that there will be exceptional circumstances where due to the risks at stake, the use of AI applications would be considered high risk as such – irrespective of

---

[253] See Ethics Guidelines for Trustworthy AI https://ec.europa.eu/futurium/en/ai-alliance-consultation/guidelines#Top The Ethics guidelines put in place 7 key requirements for the realisation of Trustworthy AI: 1) Human agency & oversight 2) Technical robustness & safety 3) Privacy & data governance 4) Transparency 5) Diversity, non-discrimination and fairness 6) Societal and environmental wellbeing and 7) Accountability

[254] Report on the safety and liability implications of Artificial Intelligence, the Internet of Things and robotic COM(2020) 64 final

[255] EU White Paper, page 15

the sector involved. Use of remote biometric identification is singled out in particular in this regard.[256]

Under the risk framework set out in the White Paper, the assessment of risk levels will depend upon the impact on affected parties. Subject to the above considerations, use of AI which may produce legal or other similarly significant effects on an individual or company, such as loss of life or limb, or is likely to deprive someone of liberty should be categorised as "*high risk*".[257]

The proposed framework focusses on several requirements for high-risk AI applications which are largely drawn from the earlier HLEG paper on ethics.

There is a recognition in the White Paper that artificial intelligence systems depend to a critical extent on the training data which is used to develop a system's skill and performance – as the White Paper itself states, "*without data, there is no AI*"[258] .

Many of the White Paper's requirements are directed at this "*data diet dependency*". So for example, there is a requirement that all datasets used to train the AI system should be sufficiently broad to cover off all relevant scenarios needed to avoid dangerous situations.

In addition, the White Paper proposes requirements which are directed at ensuring that use of AI systems does not lead to any form of prohibited discrimination. This would entail the use of training data sets that are sufficiently representative to adequately reflect all relevant gender, ethnicity and other societal factors whilst respecting core privacy and data protection principles.

The measures proposed also include requirements to keep sufficient records and data – for logically without records and evidence, it becomes

---

[256] EU White Paper, page 18

[257] EU White Paper, page 17

[258] EU White Paper, page 18

difficult to provide the evidential paper trail necessary to prove compliance. This is intended to allow the tracing back and verification of problematic AI decisions. Somewhat controversially this could conceivably extend to the relevant machine learning algorithm itself. As we have previously discussed, this might be difficult (if not impossible) to achieve with a complex "deep" learning algorithm.

The proposed requirements suggest that the following categories of data are kept: accurate records regarding the data sets used to train and test the system, including characteristics and appropriate selection criteria for the data set; the data sets themselves; and documentation on the training methodologies used to build, test and validate the AI system (including in relation to safety and steps taken to avoid bias). The white paper proposes that such information is kept for a "limited reasonable" (but unspecified) time period to ensure compliance[259].

Beyond the requirement of keeping records and data, the White Paper proposes that there is a requirement of transparency. This would entail providing clear information as to AI system capabilities, intended functioning conditions and expected levels of accuracy. It would also entail making it evident to a human user of an AI system that they are interacting with a machine and not another human. The point is made that such information should be objective, concise and easily understandable (itself a potentially tricky requirement to navigate, as we have seen in the context of the GDPR's Article 22 on Automated Decision Making[260]) and need not to be provided when it is obvious to the user that they are interacting with an AI system[261].

The White Paper then proposes requirements around robustness and accuracy. These are focussed on ensuring that AI systems are robust and accurate and at least attain the level of accuracy claimed by the system's developer. In addition to this overarching concept, there are further obligations which require reproducible outcomes (conceptually difficult in

---

[259] EU White Paper, Page 19

[260] See Chapter 3 supra on Data Protection

[261] EU White Paper, Page 20

circumstances where a deep neural network is being used – the so called "black box" that we have discussed at length earlier), those which require AI systems to "adequately" deal with what are termed "errors and inconsistencies" and those which require cyber security resilience – both against overt attacks and more subtle attempts to manipulate data or algorithms. As the extent of these requirements is largely unspecified in the White Paper, it is difficult to gauge in practice how onerous they are likely to prove.

Finally, in terms of general requirements, the White Paper focusses on the importance of human oversight. This aligns broadly with the concept of automated decision making under Article 22 of the GDPR. A number of suggestions are made as to how any such requirement could be framed – from requiring the output of the system to be approved by a human (such as in the case of a social security application) to allowing a human to intervene in a continuous AI decision making process (by e.g. pressing an "off" switch on an autonomous driving system).

The White Paper makes a special mention in relation to remote biometric identification. This is deemed to be so potentially damaging to fundamental rights that it is suggested that use should be subject to additional safeguards. Again, this aligns the proposed regulatory approach firmly with the GDPR which takes a similar regulatory stance in relation to "special category data", which includes biometric identification information. The White Paper's recommendation is that use of such data should only be authorised where such use is *"duly justified, proportionate and subject to adequate safeguards."* [262]

One issue which has caused significant conceptual difficulty in pushing AI regulation forwards has been the rather intractable problem of legal causation (discussed at length in Chapter two).

The concern here is the extent to which counterparties can be held liable for problems which may have been caused by their AI systems, especially in circumstances where, due to the *"deep"* multi-layered nature of the

---

[262] EU White Paper, page 22

tool, it is difficult, if not impossible to determine the cause of the failure.

These problems are discussed at length in an additional HLEG paper on liability (not forming part of the EU White Paper) which is highly recommended for review[263]. The White Paper itself alludes to the issues raised in detail by the HLEG Liability Paper by stating that "*in a future regulatory framework, each obligation should be addressed to the actor(s) who is (are) best placed to address any potential risks.*"[264]

What this means in effect that different actors may be responsible for different regulatory requirements at different stages of the AI product's lifecycle.

Rather counter-intuitively, the White Paper states that this should be without prejudice to which party should be liable for any damage caused under EU product law, which attributes liability to the "producer" of the product. Splitting responsibility for compliance from liability for defects (which is what the White Paper appears to be doing) seems somewhat convoluted as an approach. It should be noted however that the HLEG Liability Paper mentioned earlier discusses (rather more assertively) the possibility of potential reversals in burdens of proof in certain cases[265] and dual concepts of both Operator and Producer strict liability[266]. This may provide an insight into how future EU regulation in this space develops.

For AI which is not deemed to be "high risk", the EU proposes a voluntary labelling or certification scheme. This is intended to allow what are termed "economic operators" of the AI the right to identify their AI systems as being in conformity with agreed EU-wide benchmarks.[267]

---

[263] Liability for Artificial Intelligence and other emerging digital technologies – referred to as the HLEG Liability Paper above see https://ec.europa.eu/transparency/regexpert/index.cfm?do=groupDetail.groupMeetingDoc&docid=36608

[264] EU White Paper, page 22

[265] HLEG Liability Paper, page 52

[266] HLEG Liability Paper, pages 39 & 42

[267] EU White Paper, page 24

The UK

The UK has been keen to remain at the forefront of Artificial Intelligence development and research. In October 2017 an independent review commissioned by the UK government was published by Dame Wendy Hall and Jérôme Pesenti *"Growing the Artificial Intelligence Industry in the UK"*[268]. The review made a number of recommendations about how the UK could best exploit new technologies created by Artificial Intelligence (principally in the areas of skills, driving uptake, data security and research) and is currently being considered as part of the UK government's Industrial Strategy programme. This was followed in April 2018 by a wide ranging report by the House of Lords Select Committee on Artificial Intelligence entitled *"AI in the UK; ready, willing and able?"*[269], two of the main recommendations of which were to suggest that the AI industry set up a voluntary mechanism to inform consumers when AI is being used to make significant and sensitive decisions about individual consumers, and to ask the Law Commission to provide clarity in areas of the law where there is uncertainty around the consequences of artificial intelligence systems malfunctioning, underperforming or making decisions which cause harm[270].

ICO Auditing Framework for AI and draft ExplAIn Guidance

Since the publication of the last edition of this book, the UK's Information Commissioner has published draft guidance in conjunction with the Alan Turing institute on Explaining decisions made with AI – their so called ExplAIn Guidance[271]. This is intended to form part of their

---

[268] Available online at the Department for Digital, Culture, Media and Sport website

[269] HL Paper 100, 16th April 2018

[270] As at the date of publication, the Law Commission is only undertaking a single review on a regulatory framework for automated vehicles. See https://www.law-com.gov.uk/project/automated-vehicles/

[271] See https://ico.org.uk/media/about-the-ico/consultations/2616434/explaining-ai-decisions-part-1.pdf

Auditing Framework for AI Systems[272]. Unlike the proposed EU White Paper legislative measures, this guidance will not be enforceable as law when adopted.

Whilst it is admirable that the ICO has created this framework, which we shall examine in a little more detail shortly, it is somewhat concerning that the UK's privacy and data protection regulator has stepped into the regulatory vacuum with a focus on data.

We have seen that data forms a significant part of the value of a machine learning system, but there is a real risk in conflating personal data compliance with artificial intelligence compliance. Machine learning systems that utilise personal data will no doubt have to comply with existing data protection regulations. However artificial intelligence is so much more than data protection, and many significant or "*high risk*" (to use EU taxonomy) applications of the technology do not use personal data at all.

Significant imbalance in the regulatory spectrum is created if emphasis is skewed towards applications that utilise personal data as against those that don't. As I have mentioned elsewhere in other publications, it should not be correct that an autonomous vehicle that has the ability to potentially kill or maim road users should be regulated in a less rigorous way than a machine learning system that screens individuals for loan eligibility.

The upshot of this is that Data protection compliance for machine learning systems is not a substitutable replacement for a fully thought-out regulatory framework for artificial intelligence technologies and should neither be treated nor held out as such.

In this regard the EU's considered approach as set out in its White Paper at least applies that conceptual rigour, recognising the crucial interaction between privacy and AI regulatory issues. One of the weaknesses of the UK ICO's framework and guidance is that it trivialises this distinction for readers that are not fully versed in the technology[273].

---

[272] See https://ico.org.uk/about-the-ico/news-and-events/ai-blog-an-overview-of-the-auditing-framework-for-artificial-intelligence-and-its-core-components/

[273] See for example a comment on page 7 of part 1 of the ExplAIn guidance "*where AI does not involve the use of personal data, it falls outside the remit of data protection*

The Auditing framework for AI[274] was released by ICO on 14th February 2020 and is intended to put in place a non-binding risk based "best practice" framework for the evaluation, use and adoption of artificial intelligence-based systems, albeit with an exclusive focus on data protection issues. It also proposes a methodology to audit AI applications and provides guidance on the preparation of context specific data protection impact assessments. Usefully the Auditing framework also refers to and provides a critical examination of the inevitable trade-offs that need to be made between system efficiency and privacy compliant standards, most particularly in the areas of bias and discrimination[275].

ICO's ExplAIn draft guidance was issued subject to a consultation period which closed in January 2020. As at the date of writing of this book, the COVID-19 pandemic has delayed publication of the final version of this guidance.

Part one of the ICO's ExplAIn guidance sets out the reasons why from a data protection perspective, it is important to provide an explanation for decisions made by machine learning systems. This reiterates the basic principles of automated decision making under Article 22 of the GDPR (requiring human in the loop decision making absent explicit consent) together with the requirements of Articles 13, 14 & 15 of the GDPR (requiring the provision of meaningful information about the logic involved in the decision). These have already been discussed at length[276]. The draft guidance also refers to Recital 71 of the GDPR which refers to a right to "an explanation" of an automated decision[277]. After setting out the proposed benefits and risks of providing such explanations, the guidance suggests that there are six main types of explanation that should be

---

law. For example, the use of AI for weather forecasting or astronomy."

[274] See https://ico.org.uk/media/about-the-ico/consultations/2617219/guidance-on-the-ai-auditing-framework-draft-for-consultation.pdf

[275] See Page 26 of the AI Auditing Framework draft guidance

[276] See Chapter 3, supra

[277] The ICO Guidance states that "*The GDPR's recitals are not legally binding but they do clarify the meaning and intention of its articles...Recital 71 makes clear that such a right is implicit in Articles 15 and 22*".

provided depending on the AI use case and context[278], although not necessarily separately. There are four separate core principles advocated in the guidance which are intended to drive the way in which appropriate explanations are given: *Be transparent; Be accountable; Consider context* and *Reflect on Impacts*.[279]

Part Two of the draft ExplAIn guidance[280] focusses on the provision of more practical guidance for the provision of appropriate explanations for AI decision making, whilst Part Three[281] looks at explanations from the perspective of enterprise: that is to say, who should be responsible for the provision of appropriate explanations within an organisation.

Unfortunately the way in which the guidance is prepared does little to avoid the conflation risk highlighted earlier – overemphasising data protection risks with the net result that there is likely to be an excessive focus on personal data and GDPR related issues when attempting to follow the guidance's stated "best practice".

Two further consultations in the UK are worthy of being mentioned, although it is currently too early to provide any definitive commentary on outcomes. The first is a recently closed consultation by the UK Intellectual Property office on the potential impact of artificial intelligence on the UK's intellectual property regime[282] – this ran from 7th September 2020 to 30th November and is currently being considered by the UK IPO, and the second is a consultation on the potential trade related harms caused by algorithms being carried out by the UK's Competition and

---

[278] A *Rationale* explanation; a *Responsibility* explanation; a *Data* explanation; a *Fairness* explanation; a *Safety and Performance* explanation and an *Impact* explanation. See page 19 of Part 1 of the guidance, et seq.

[279] See page 24 of Part 1 of the guidance, et seq.

[280] See https://ico.org.uk/media/about-the-ico/consultations/2616433/explaining-ai-decisions-part-2.pdf

[281] See https://ico.org.uk/media/about-the-ico/consultations/2616436/explaining-ai-decisions-part-3.pdf

[282] See https://www.gov.uk/government/consultations/artificial-intelligence-and-intellectual-property-call-for-views

Markets Authority[283]. This opened on 19th January 2021 and, as at the date of publication is due to close on 16th March 2021.

The United States

CCPA – California Consumer Privacy Act 2018

The CCPA was passed by the California State Legislature in 2018[284]. This was a major milestone by California in its privacy regime which has particular significance to the high technology industries of the United States given the predominance of Silicon Valley as a tech industry hub. Broadly speaking, the CCPA introduces a new set of consumer privacy rights analogous to those within the GDPR, including rights to be informed of processing, the right to opt-out of processing and the right to deletion of data but does not contain the proscriptive provisions on automated processing[285] contained in the EU measure. As such it presents less of a challenge to AI system usage than the GDPR.

Executive Order 13859

In February 2019, the US Presidency issued Executive Order 13859 on *"Maintaining American Leadership in Artificial Intelligence"*[286]. The Executive Order mandates continued American AI leadership in the research, development and deployment of AI and puts in place a co-ordinated federal "whole of government" strategy based on five guiding principles[287].

---

[283] See https://www.gov.uk/government/consultations/algorithms-competition-and-consumer-harm-call-for-information

[284] See https://leginfo.legislature.ca.gov/faces/billTextClient.xhtml?bill_id=201720180AB375

[285] Article 22 – see Chapter three

[286] See https://www.federalregister.gov/documents/2019/02/14/2019-02544/maintaining-american-leadership-in-artificial-intelligence

[287] These are summarised as follows: (a) drive technological breakthroughs in AI; (b) drive development of appropriate technical standards and reduce barriers to the safe testing and deployment of AI technologies; (c) train American workers with the skills to develop and apply AI technologies; (d) foster public trust and confidence in AI technologies and protect civil liberties, privacy, and American values in their application; and (e) promote an international environment that supports

Federal agencies that are deemed to be "implementing" agencies for the purposes of the Order[288] are required to co-ordinate strategic objectives in relation to their development and use of AI.

Whilst the Order itself does not specifically lay down any regulations in relation to AI applications, it tasked the OMB[289] Director with responsibility for the preparation of a memorandum to the heads of government agencies informing them of the approved regulatory oversight they should be taking in relation to AI developed and deployed outside of the Federal Government, consistent with the strategy set in the Executive Order. Specifically this memo is required to be issued in draft form for consultation by the public prior to finalisation.

Draft OMB Memorandum on AI Regulation

The OMB Memo was released on 7th January 2020 and was subject to a 60-day public consultation period. It limits itself to non-governmental use and to narrow or "weak" AI.

Specifically the memo declares that *"Agencies must avoid a precautionary approach that holds AI systems to such an impossibly high standard that society cannot enjoy their benefits"*[290]. The memo sets out ten guiding principles for the stewardship of AI applications[291].

American AI research and innovation and opens markets for American AI industries, while protecting critical AI technologies from acquisition by strategic competitors and adversarial nations.

[288] See section 3 of the Executive Order

[289] Office of Management and Budget

[290] See Page 2 of the draft OMB memo, under "Encouraging Innovation and Growth in AI"

[291] These are set out on page 3 and are in summary 1) Public Trust in AI; 2) Public Participation; 3) Scientific Integrity and Information Quality; 4) Risk Assessment and Management; 5) Benefits and Cost; 6) Flexibility; 7) Fairness and Non-Discrimination; 8) Disclosure and Transparency; 9) Safety and Security and 10) Inter-agency Coordination.

The principles themselves direct agencies to a non-interventionist approach balancing risks and benefits[292], and in particular tasks agencies with a comparison of such new AI systems as against the costs and benefits of existing legacy systems they are designed to replace when assessing the need for regulation.

---

[292] *"Agencies should consider new regulation only after they have reached the decision…that Federal regulation is necessary…"* page 3 of the Memo – See also principle 5 on Benefits and Costs

MORE BOOKS BY
LAW BRIEF PUBLISHING

A selection of our other titles available now:-

'A Practical Guide to Solicitor and Client Costs – 2nd Edition' by Robin Dunne
'Constructive Dismissal – Practice Pointers and Principles' by Benjimin Burgher
'A Practical Guide to Religion and Belief Discrimination Claims in the Workplace' by Kashif Ali
'A Practical Guide to the Law of Medical Treatment Decisions' by Ben Troke
'Fundamental Dishonesty and QOCS in Personal Injury Proceedings: Law and Practice' by Jake Rowley
'A Practical Guide to the Law in Relation to School Exclusions' by Charlotte Hadfield & Alice de Coverley
'A Practical Guide to Divorce for the Silver Separators' by Karin Walker
'The Right to be Forgotten – The Law and Practical Issues' by Melissa Stock
'A Practical Guide to Planning Law and Rights of Way in National Parks, the Broads and AONBs' by James Maurici QC, James Neill et al
'A Practical Guide to Election Law' by Tom Tabori
'A Practical Guide to the Law in Relation to Surrogacy' by Andrew Powell
'A Practical Guide to Claims Arising from Fatal Accidents – 2nd Edition' by James Patience
'A Practical Guide to the Ownership of Employee Inventions – From Entitlement to Compensation' by James Tumbridge & Ashley Roughton
'A Practical Guide to Asbestos Claims' by Jonathan Owen & Gareth McAloon
'A Practical Guide to Stamp Duty Land Tax in England and Northern Ireland' by Suzanne O'Hara
'A Practical Guide to the Law of Farming Partnerships' by Philip Whitcomb

'Covid-19, Homeworking and the Law – The Essential Guide to Employment and GDPR Issues' by Forbes Solicitors

'Covid-19, Force Majeure and Frustration of Contracts – The Essential Guide' by Keith Markham

'Covid-19 and Criminal Law – The Essential Guide' by Ramya Nagesh

'Covid-19 and Family Law in England and Wales – The Essential Guide' by Safda Mahmood

'A Practical Guide to the Law of Unlawful Eviction and Harassment – 2nd Edition' by Stephanie Lovegrove

'Covid-19, Residential Property, Equity Release and Enfranchisement – The Essential Guide' by Paul Sams and Louise Uphill

'Covid-19, Brexit and the Law of Commercial Leases – The Essential Guide' by Mark Shelton

'A Practical Guide to Costs in Personal Injury Claims – 2nd Edition' by Matthew Hoe

'A Practical Guide to the General Data Protection Regulation (GDPR) – 2nd Edition' by Keith Markham

'Ellis on Credit Hire – Sixth Edition' by Aidan Ellis & Tim Kevan

'A Practical Guide to Working with Litigants in Person and McKenzie Friends in Family Cases' by Stuart Barlow

'Protecting Unregistered Brands: A Practical Guide to the Law of Passing Off' by Lorna Brazell

'A Practical Guide to Secondary Liability and Joint Enterprise Post-Jogee' by Joanne Cecil & James Mehigan

'A Practical Guide to the Pre-Action RTA Claims Protocol for Personal Injury Lawyers' by Antonia Ford

'A Practical Guide to Neighbour Disputes and the Law' by Alexander Walsh

'A Practical Guide to Forfeiture of Leases' by Mark Shelton

'A Practical Guide to Coercive Control for Legal Practitioners and Victims' by Rachel Horman

These books and more are available to order online direct from the publisher at www.lawbriefpublishing.com, where you can also read free sample chapters. For any queries, contact us on 0844 587 2383 or mail@lawbriefpublishing.com.

Our books are also usually in stock at www.amazon.co.uk with free next day delivery for Prime members, and at good legal bookshops such as Wildy & Sons.

We are regularly launching new books in our series of practical day-to-day practitioners' guides. Visit our website and join our free newsletter to be kept informed and to receive special offers, free chapters, etc.

You can also follow us on Twitter at www.twitter.com/lawbriefpub.

Lightning Source UK Ltd.
Milton Keynes UK
UKHW020923121121
393851UK00006BA/336

9 781912 687787